...egic ...nce ...ew

...pporting Essays

London : The Stationery Office   £14.95

Produced by the Directorate of Defence Policy
Design and Artwork by MOD Central Services (Media) Graphics London
Printed in the UK for the Stationery Office Limited on behalf of the
Controller of Her Majesty's Stationery Office
Dd 5068142, 7/98, 3840, Job No. 0052138

THE STRATEGIC DEFENCE REVIEW
SUPPORTING ESSAYS

FOREWORD BY THE SECRETARY OF STATE FOR DEFENCE
The Rt. Hon. GEORGE ROBERTSON MP

1.   At the beginning of the Strategic Defence Review, I said that I wanted our conclusions "to have been formed and tested in a wider forum". The result was a unique process of consultation with the widest possible range of expertise in defence and related areas. This was the most open re-examination of Britain's defence ever conducted.

2.   Throughout the Review, I have been determined to extend the principle of openness, to reflect this Government's commitment to open Government and to encourage informed debate on all aspects of our defence policy. The Strategic Defence Review White Paper sets out the main themes of our work and the main conclusions we have reached. It cannot, however, address issues or explain the background to our conclusions in great detail.

3.   I have therefore commissioned this volume of essays, which fills in these details for the key strands of the Review. It is not comprehensive; our work covered so much ground that this would be impossible. But it does address what I believe to be the main aspects of this work. In some respects, including the essay on the policy framework, it reflects very closely the papers considered by Ministers. I am also taking this opportunity to publish for the first time the Ministry of Defence's objectives.

4.   The Strategic Defence Review set out to provide Britain's Armed Forces with a new sense of clarity, coherence and consensus. This volume of essays will, I believe, demonstrate how we achieved our goal and contribute towards a much wider shared vision of Britain's security needs.

Ministry of Defence
July 1998

MINISTRY OF DEFENCE OBJECTIVES

Objectives

The objectives of the Ministry of Defence are to provide the defence capabilities needed:

– to ensure the security and defence of the United Kingdom and the Overseas Territories, including against terrorism;

– to support the Government's foreign policy objectives, particularly in promoting international peace and security.

Supporting Objectives (grouped by outputs)

Department of State:

– to produce a defence strategy, policy and programme matched to our security needs now and in the future;

– to help dispel hostility and to build and maintain trust through defence diplomacy, and to play an effective and leading part in support of NATO, the Western European Union and the United Nations;

– to provide clear and timely strategic direction on the participation of UK forces in conflict prevention, crisis management and operations;

– to allocate available resources in the way which maximises military capability and other Departmental outputs;

– to encourage the competitive strengths of British defence suppliers and, within the framework of the Government's arms sales policy, to support British defence exports.

Military Capability:

– to bring together maritime, ground and air components into coherent joint forces under unified command fully capable of achieving the Government's strategic objectives;

– to deliver appropriately motivated, manned, trained and equipped force packages, at the required level of readiness, and with the necessary support, sustainability and deployability, to achieve the full range of agreed military tasks.

Equipment Programme:

– to procure equipment which most cost-effectively meets agreed military requirements.

Success in achieving these objectives depends upon:

– being a good, equal-opportunity employer offering a clear sense of purpose and able to attract recruits and retain well-trained personnel;

– seeking value for money in every activity of the MOD and the Services;

– communicating effectively, internally and externally, why defence matters and the tasks of our forces and the civilian personnel who work with them.

SUPPORTING ESSAY ONE
THE STRATEGIC DEFENCE REVIEW PROCESS

The Aim of the Review

1.   The Strategic Defence Review was announced in the Queen's Speech on 14 May 1997, and subsequently launched by the Defence Secretary at a press conference on 28 May:

> "Its aim is clear cut; to build on the developing consensus on defence and to establish the widest possible shared vision about Britain's future security needs and the tasks of its Armed Forces . . . . to provide Britain's Armed Forces with a new sense of clarity, coherence and consensus."

The Nature of the Review

2.   It was fundamental to the Government's approach that the Review would be foreign policy-led. The Ministry of Defence and the Foreign and Commonwealth Office would work together to establish a policy framework upon which the Review would build. The process would be open and inclusive, not conducted in secret behind closed doors. It would include consultation with the widest possible range of outside expertise and opinion. More generally, the Defence Secretary encouraged and welcomed suggestions and ideas from any source. He explained that:

> "I want our conclusions to have been formed and tested in a wider forum, and to be accepted as the right defence policy for Britain . . . . No-one should be able to claim at the end of the Review that they were not given the opportunity to have their say."

Parameters

3.   The Review did not start with a blank piece of paper, but operated within parameters set out in the Government's General Election manifesto, including strong defence, security based on NATO, and retention of Trident combined with multinational arms control. The Defence Secretary also stressed the vital importance of people:

> ". . . . although our ships, tanks and jet fighters may appear impressive, it is the men and women who operate, maintain and support them who really make the difference. This Government will give its full support to Service personnel, their families, and our civilian staff."

4.   Within these guidelines, the Review took a fresh look at all aspects of defence policy and programmes.

Structure

5.   The Review was conducted in overlapping stages as shown in *FIGURE 1.*

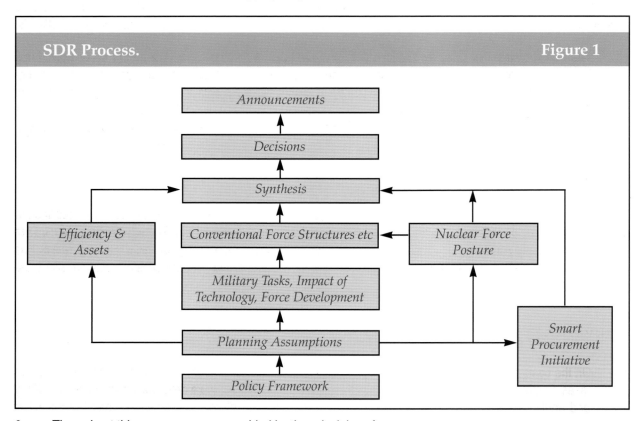

SDR Process.   **Figure 1**

6.   Throughout this process, we were guided by the principles of:

   – openness – keeping our own people, Parliament, our Allies and partners, the wider defence community and the public in touch with progress;

   – maximum use of existing structures – drawing on the expertise of our in-house staff, rather than setting up a separate Review team;

   – the widest possible involvement within the Ministry of Defence, the Government as a whole and more widely.

7.   Most of the work was carried out in working groups, comprising military and civilian personnel and representatives of other Government Departments, under an overall structure managed by the Vice Chief of the Defence Staff and the Second Permanent Secretary. Examples of the working groups are at Annex A. The results at each stage were synthesised for discussion by a range of senior committees, up to and including the Defence Council. This approach was based firmly on the principles set out above, drawing upon the Department's existing structures and working practices where appropriate.

The Policy Framework

8.   The first stage of the Review was conducted jointly by the Ministry of Defence and the Foreign and Commonwealth Office. It assessed our national interests, commitments and responsibilities, and considered potential risks and challenges in the decades ahead, and set out the overall role of defence in support of Britain's foreign and

security policy, to provide the framework for subsequent stages of the Review. This work is summarised in the essay on the Policy Framework.

9.   To inform this work and test emerging conclusions, the Foreign and Defence Secretaries held two open seminars on 3 and 11 July 1997, in London and Coventry. These were attended by Members of Parliament, academics, representatives of non-Governmental organisations, and the media, in addition to Ministers and officials.

10.   The Policy Framework was endorsed by Ministers as a basis for further work. We subsequently considered publishing it as a separate document. But our conclusion was that this work could not easily be separated out from the Review's later stages. The Defence Secretary decided nonetheless that it would be right to make public the broad conclusions we had reached so far, and the main themes were set out in his speech to the Royal United Services Institute on 18 September 1997, and in the Defence Debate in the House of Commons on 27 and 28 October 1997.

Planning Assumptions

11.   Planning assumptions convert policy into detailed guidance for defence planning. They cover the activities our forces need to be able to undertake, and the context in which they will undertake them. The assumptions then inform further work to identify the specific force structures, capabilities, equipment and support required. This phase was carried out in broadly-based working groups. The main elements of the planning assumptions are summarised in the essay on Future Military Capabilities.

Conventional Forces

12.   On the basis of the planning assumptions, our requirements for conventional forces were considered, in two main phases. Firstly, the eight missions identified by the planning assumptions were developed further into 28 Military Tasks, and additional work was carried out on the future development of specific capabilities and the impact of technology on future military equipment and capability. This work was again conducted in working groups, and took account of external submissions made to the Review and a third seminar, held in the Ministry of Defence Main Building in November and attended by outside experts and members of the public.

13.   The second phase assessed the forces, capabilities, equipment and support needed to conduct the Missions and Military Tasks. It was by some margin the largest phase of the Review. The working group structure was retained, but a number of senior officers and officials were given responsibility for ensuring that the work of the groups rigorously analysed the issues and considered imaginatively the options which might be pursued. Ministers directed that no options should be ruled out.

14.   The process was iterative, with issues and options considered at various stages by senior committees and Ministers, including a Steering Group chaired by the Minister of State for the Armed Forces. Once the full range of options had been established they were costed. The outcome of this phase of the Review is covered in most of the following essays.

Nuclear Forces

15.   The Government's undertaking to retain Trident provided one of the pillars of the Review. Against this background, work on nuclear forces reassessed all aspects of our nuclear deterrent posture in the light of our essential security interests and defence needs. Working groups looked at the long term worst case requirement over the lifetime of Trident and considered how our nuclear deterrent capabilities and requirements for conventional supporting forces

could be adjusted to meet Britain's needs in the changed strategic environment. Their conclusions are addressed in detail in the essay on Deterrence, Arms Control and Proliferation.

Procurement Policy

16.   On 30 July 1997, the Defence Secretary announced that the Strategic Defence Review would include a "Smart Procurement" initiative to ensure that future equipment procurement was faster, cheaper and better. Ministry of Defence staff worked with industry to identify a package of measures to lead to speedier, more coherent processes, improve the operation of the Department's internal organisations and mechanisms, and improve its relationship with industry.

17.   In order to get maximum benefit from Smart Procurement, the initiative included a fundamental review of the process by which MOD acquires equipment, and the way the Department is organised to conduct that process. Every facet of the procurement process was examined, drawing on a wide range of outside expertise and experience, including the National Defence Industries Council and Trade Associations. There was also an open seminar at Didcot. Work was overseen by a Ministerial Group chaired by the Parliamentary Under Secretary of State, and is described in the essay on Procurement and Industry.

Efficiency and Assets

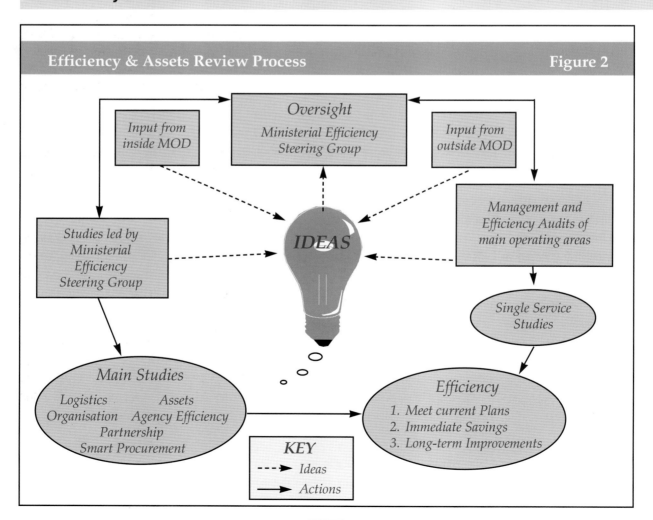

Efficiency & Assets Review Process — Figure 2

18.   Although the Review was firmly policy-led, it also took a hard look at how the Department could ensure best value for money from defence resources. Every area of defence business was examined with the aim of seeking out new efficiency savings. One of the main aims was to make financial headroom so that we could rectify shortfalls in capability and meet new requirements identified in other areas of the Review. To this end, a specific strand of work was established to maximise the efficiency of our organisational structures and working practices, especially in the support area. This work was overseen by the Ministerial Efficiency Steering Group chaired by the Minister of State for the Armed Forces. The process is illustrated in *FIGURE 2* and is described in detail in the essay on Support and Infrastructure.

External Inputs to the Review

19.   Ministers directed that maximum use should be made of the knowledge and expertise of our military and civilian staff. To reinforce this, we actively sought ideas and suggestions from all sources. The aim was an open, inclusive Review which would encourage a better informed debate on defence issues and help build a wide consensus on defence policy.

20.   The Strategic Defence Review was a unique exercise in consultation on defence. In addition to the open seminars described elsewhere in this essay, the Secretary of State invited anyone with an interest in or a view on defence to make a submission to the process. Over five hundred submissions were received, from MPs and Peers, local authorities, academics, industry, interest groups, journalists, and members of the public. They were circulated to staff dealing with the subjects to which the submissions related. All were interesting and some had a significant impact on our work. Correspondents received an acknowledgement and will receive substantive replies in the light of the results of the Review.

21.   Submissions were also encouraged from Service and civilian personnel, to ensure that we took advantage of the experience and imagination of staff who might not be directly involved in any of the Review's work processes. About a hundred such submissions were received.

22.   In a related initiative, the Secretary of State set up a panel of eighteen outsiders with a range of interests and experience in defence and other areas. His purpose was to seek advice from different perspectives, and to test the conclusions emerging from the work. Several of the members also made valuable contributions to the work on efficiency, assets and procurement. Membership of the expert panel is shown at Annex B to this essay.

23.   To spread the net even more widely, a series of informal discussions was held with former Defence Ministers, retired senior officers and officials, industrialists, trade unionists, academics, former and current MPs, Peers, scientists, non-Governmental organisations and environmentalists. These occasions promoted free and wide ranging discussion, and the views expressed were fed into our work. *FIGURE 3* shows the inputs to the SDR.

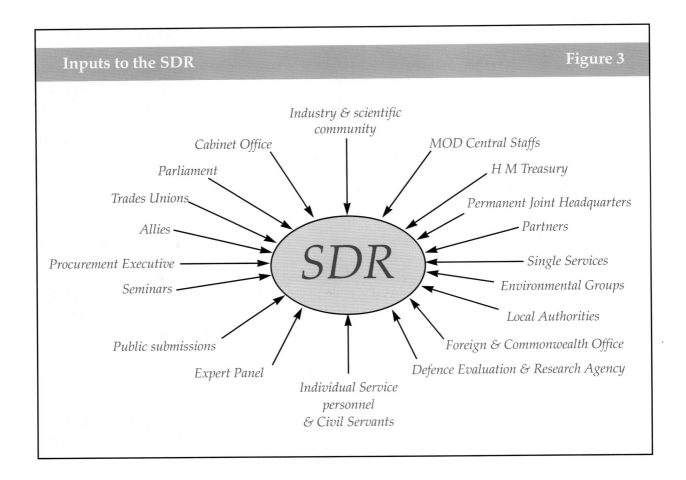

Inputs to the SDR

Figure 3

Consultation and Information

24. The Department sought to maintain a two-way flow of information on the Review with all interested parties. Parliament had opportunities to express views, in the House of Commons Defence Debate on 27 and 28 October 1997, and in the House of Lords on 6 November. There was also an adjournment debate in the House of Commons on 25 February 1998. Copies of outside inputs were placed in the libraries of both Houses of Parliament (subject to their authors' consent). The House of Commons Defence Committee received briefings to keep them up-to-date with emerging findings. During this period, Defence Ministers also answered over one hundred and fifty Parliamentary Questions on the Review, in addition to correspondence and enquiries from MPs and Peers.

25. From the outset we were committed to keep our NATO Allies and other partners informed of what was happening. The NATO and WEU Secretary Generals, Defence Ministers of NATO Allies, and Five Power Defence Arrangements and Gulf Co-operation Council countries were all kept informed in letters, and at a broad range of NATO and bilateral meetings.

26. Throughout the Review process a range of methods were used to keep the wider public in touch with progress. The Defence Secretary made keynote speeches at the Royal United Services Institute on 18 September 1997 and at Chatham House on 12 March 1998, and wrote an article for *The Independent* on 30 July 1997. Regular press releases were given to the national and regional press, and the text of key speeches and summaries of the seminars were made available on the Ministry of Defence Internet site *[http://www.mod.uk]*. A BBC television documentary on the process was broadcast on 31 May.

27. To keep Service and civilian staff up to date regular articles were published in our various in-house journals. These were supplemented in February 1998 by a short leaflet issued to all personnel with their pay-slips.

28. A key part of the consultation process was the establishment of a liaison team to talk directly to military and civilian personnel throughout defence. The team was led by a Group Captain and included representatives from all three Services and the Civil Service. They listened personally to views expressed by individuals at all levels, who were encouraged to speak frankly, and reports were made directly to the Defence Secretary. It was impossible for the team to speak to every employee, but their visit programme provided over 7,500 staff with an opportunity to discuss the Review and make their views known. It also gave Ministers a valuable insight into many of the issues of most immediate concern to Service personnel and civilian staff.

29. The MOD engaged the Trade Unions fully in this process of consultation. They were invited to put forward general views at the outset, and officials kept them informed of developments throughout the Review, including through the MOD Whitley Council machinery. Trade Unionists were also actively involved in other aspects of the consultation process, including informal meetings and seminars. In March 1998 the Trade Unions were given a broad indication of emerging conclusions, and this was followed up with a meeting with the Defence Secretary on 7 April 1998 where they were able to feed in their views before decisions were taken. When final decisions are implemented the Trade Unions will be fully consulted in accordance with normal Departmental procedures.

Synthesis and Decision-Making

30. Options generated by the Review were submitted to Ministers after consideration by the various official bodies described above. Other Government Departments remained involved in this process, including through an inter-departmental group chaired by the Cabinet Office.

31. In the early part of 1998, the Defence Secretary held a series of meetings with his Ministerial colleagues, the Chiefs of Staff and senior officials, to consider the costed options identified by the working groups and to discuss the issues with those who had led the work in each case. The purpose of these meetings was not to take immediate decisions, but to discuss the issues with senior advisers, particularly the Chiefs of Staff, to commission further work where required and, progressively, to rule out options.

32. This rolling process enabled the Defence Secretary to ensure that the working groups had addressed the issues rigorously and imaginatively, and that the inter-connections between them had been properly identified and understood. As a result, the Defence Secretary and his most senior advisers were able to put together a coherent package of measures.

33. The Defence Secretary submitted these proposals to the Prime Minister on 27 March 1998. They formed both the output of the Strategic Defence Review and the MOD's input to the Government-wide Comprehensive Spending Review.

Announcement

34. We aimed to announce the conclusions of the Review as widely as possible. The main vehicles were a White Paper setting out the Government's defence policy and plans, and this volume of supporting essays. Allies and partners were fully briefed, and the Review's conclusions were also issued through press releases to national and regional press, set out in writing to a similarly wide range of people as contributed to the Review, and lodged on the Internet. Particular importance was attached to the internal MOD and Government wide announcements. Within MOD,

4,500 packs of information containing specially written information sheets were prepared to inform military and civilian staff of the main conclusions of the Review and how those conclusions would affect their particular area of business. Much effort was made to ensure that internal briefing followed as closely as possible on announcements in Parliament.

Conclusion

35.   This foreign policy-led, open and inclusive process clearly distinguishes the Strategic Defence Review from previous reviews. The results demonstrate the value of harnessing the knowledge, experience and ideas of the many rather than the few. We believe that this approach has produced a clear and coherent future for Britain's defence, and one which should command a broad consensus, not only amongst defence professionals but with the British public and our friends abroad.

Annex A to SDR Process Essay

EXAMPLES OF WORKING GROUPS

Planning Assumptions –
* future defence missions
* Allies and other partners
* potential theatres of operations
* capabilities of potential future adversaries
* scale and concurrency of operations
* readiness requirements
* sustainability and recuperation
* basing issues
* military crisis management
* rapid deployment forces and NATO reaction forces

Force Structures and Capabilities –

Nuclear Forces, including
* warhead and missile requirements
* Trident submarine operating posture
* nuclear disarmament/arms control
* fissile material management
* future warhead capability programme

Conventional Forces –

Utility of the present and planned force structure in relation to planning assumptions and military tasks, together with studies into specific areas such as:
* underpinning defence diplomacy
* a British contribution to UN standing forces
* Caribbean Presence
* Search and Rescue/Fishery protection

Size, shape and readiness, including:
* Force Structure requirements, particularly to provide Joint Rapid Reaction Forces
* Readiness
* Reserve structures
* Training and operational cycles and levels of separated service

Logistics Support, including:

* Logistics support to expeditionary and joint operations

* Sustainability

Organisation and Basing, including:

* Army Organisation

* Basing of the Army in the UK and Germany

* Command and Control of Contingency Forces

* Ground-based air defence and Nuclear Biological and Chemical defence

* Organisation of battlefield helicopters

Forward Equipment Issues, including:

* The forward equipment programme

* Strategic Lift

* Carrier-based aircraft, carriers and future offensive air systems

* Information and communication systems

* Future medium surface to air missile & ballistic missile defence

The return on our Investment in People

Annex B to SDR Process Essay

MEMBERSHIP OF THE EXPERT PANEL

* **Sir Michael Alexander** (UK Ambassador to NATO 1986-92, Chairman of RUSI)

* **Janet Bruce, Lady Balfour of Burleigh** (Consultant and Author, including Editor of The Diaries of a Cabinet Minister 1964-70 by Richard Crossman; Chairman of Cable and Wireless Resource Ltd.)

* **Janet Cohen** (Director of Charterhouse Bank Ltd and Governor of the BBC)

* **Professor Lawrence Freedman** (Professor of War Studies, King's College, University of London)

* **Air Marshal Sir Timothy Garden** (Former Assistant Chief of the Air Staff, now Director of the Royal Institute of International Affairs)

* **Lord Gladwin of Clee** (Former Regional Secretary GMWU; Member of the Employment Appeals Tribunal)

* **Dr. James Gow** (King's College, University of London; Expert Advisor to the Office of the Prosecutor, International Criminal Tribunal for the Former Yugoslavia (1994-97))

* **Professor Colin Gray** (Director of Security Studies, University of Hull; Formerly Director of National Security Studies at the Hudson Institute, New York)

* **Simon Jenkins** (Columnist of the Year 1993; Columnist for The Times and the London Evening Standard and formerly Editor of both newspapers)

* **Richard Lapthorne** (Vice Chairman of British Aerospace plc and member of the Industrial Development Advisory Board)

* **Dr. Patricia Lewis** (Formerly Director of the Verification Technology Information Centre (VERTIC); now Director of The United Nations Institute for Disarmament Research (UNIDIR))

* **Admiral of the Fleet Sir Julian Oswald** (Chief of the Naval Staff 1989-93; currently Chairman of Aerosystems International)

* **Trevor Phillips** (Presenter of LWT's The London Programme, and weekly Columnist for The Independent)

* **Sir Michael Quinlan** (Director of the Ditchley Foundation; formerly Permanent Secretary at the Ministry of Defence 1988-92)

* **John Rose** (Chief Executive of Rolls Royce plc)

*   **Dr. Alan Rudge** (Chairman, WS Atkins plc; Chairman of The Engineering and Physical Sciences Research Council; Chairman of The Engineering Council; and Chairman of ERA Technology Ltd.)

*   **Colonel Terence Taylor** (Assistant Director of the International Institute of Strategic Studies and Editor of *The Military Balance*)

*   **Field Marshal the Lord Vincent** (Chief of the Defence Staff 1991-2, Chairman of the NATO Military Committee 1993-96)

SUPPORTING ESSAY TWO
THE POLICY FRAMEWORK

1.   The Government's General Election Manifesto said that we would conduct a Strategic Defence Review "to reassess our essential security interests and defence needs [and] consider how the roles, missions and capabilities of the armed forces should be adjusted to meet the new strategic realities". The starting point was the Government's Manifesto commitments to a strong defence against post-Cold War security challenges, security based on NATO, retention of the nuclear deterrent combined with progress on arms control, and a strong defence industry.

2.   The Review has been foreign policy-led and the first stage, conducted jointly by the Foreign and Commonwealth Office and the MOD, provided the policy framework for subsequent work. Its analysis and conclusions, which are summarised in this essay, were tested against a range of outside views, including in two open seminars.

3.   For most of the post-war period, British defence planning was dominated by countering the massive threat from the Soviet Union and by the withdrawal from our overseas empire. There was little foreign policy choice in how we organised our security. That situation has been transformed by the end of the Cold War and by the new co-operative partnership with Russia and the countries of Central and Eastern Europe. The disappearance of the Soviet threat was a result, in part, of the effective system for collective defence in Europe which we played a key role in creating and maintaining. NATO has evolved to become a positive force for stability and confidence for the whole of Europe. We now have a real opportunity to devise a security posture which will support and underpin all Britain's interests overseas, in a world where democracy and liberal economic systems continue to spread.

4.   The new challenges we face will call for the combined application of all the tools at our disposal - diplomatic, economic, trade, developmental, as well as the Armed Forces. In the changed world there is a new and growing role for preventive diplomacy which brings all these tools to bear to avert conflict before military intervention is required. However, this essay necessarily focuses on the defence dimension.

Interests

5.   Britain's place in the world is determined by our interests as a nation and as a leading member of the international community. The two are inextricably linked because our national interests have a vital international dimension.

6.   Britain is a major European state and a leading member of the European Union (EU). Our economic and political future is as part of Europe. British security is indivisible from that of our European partners and allies. We therefore have a fundamental interest in the security and stability of the continent as a whole, and in the effectiveness of NATO as a collective political and military instrument to underpin these interests.

7.   Our economy is founded on international trade. Exports form a higher proportion of Gross Domestic Product than for the US, Japan, Germany or France. We invest more of our income abroad than any major economy. Our closest economic partners are the EU and the US but our investment in the developing world amounts to the combined total of France, Germany and Italy. Foreign investment into the UK also provides nearly 20% of manufacturing jobs.

8.   British economic interests and our history give us other international responsibilities. Over ten million British citizens live and work overseas. We have 13 Overseas Territories spread around the world. We are members of many important international organisations and have developed close ties of friendship with countries in every continent. And as an open society, we are easily affected by global trends and other external influences.

9.   A nation's foreign policy must reflect its values. Britain stands for a strong world community, where differences are resolved fairly and peacefully. Our national security and prosperity thus depend on promoting international stability, freedom and economic development. As a Permanent Member of the United Nations Security Council, Britain

is both willing and able to play a leading role internationally. We have a responsibility to contribute to a strong world community. But we cannot achieve all our aims alone. Instead, we need to work through strong partnerships and alliances, particularly the EU and NATO. We also attach immense importance to the international community as a whole working together through the UN and other international organisations.

10.   This is summed up in the four broad foreign policy goals outlined by the Foreign and Commonwealth Secretary on 12 May 1997:

> **<u>Security</u> of the United Kingdom and Overseas Territories and peace for our people by promoting international stability, fostering our defence alliances and promoting arms control;**
>
> **<u>Prosperity</u>, promoting trade and jobs at home, and combating poverty and promoting sustained development overseas;**
>
> **<u>Quality of Life</u>, protecting the world's environment and countering the menace of drugs, terrorism and crime;**
>
> **<u>Mutual Respect</u>, spreading the values of human rights, civil liberties and democracy which we demand for ourselves.**

Security Priorities

Support to the Civil Power

11.   Support to the Civil Power in Northern Ireland has been a major task for our Armed Forces. The future of Northern Ireland must be determined with the consent of the people. The Government is committed to reconciliation between the two traditions and to a political settlement which commands the support of both. The Good Friday Peace Process marks a new beginning in this respect and the Government is committed to its success. We must, however, maintain the ability to combat terrorism of all kinds throughout the United Kingdom.

Europe

12.   Changes over the last decade have radically improved the security context for Britain, but the collapse of Yugoslavia has shown how instability in Europe can escalate into conflict and spill over borders. Collective security based on NATO, the transatlantic link, and the continuing development of a more effective European Security and Defence Identity in NATO through the WEU, continue to offer the best guarantee of deterring and insuring against new security risks in Europe.

13.   Our military and political contribution to NATO is effective and highly valued. But because of increased operational commitments in support of foreign policy, many areas of our forces are now suffering from severe overstretch, with unprecedented short gaps between operational tours. This has effects on morale and retention.

14.   It will remain in our interests to continue to play a leading role in the Alliance. If our contribution fell significantly, NATO's ability to undertake crisis management and peace support effectively would be reduced, our ability to influence NATO in ways which reinforce our security would decline and we would send a dangerous message to the US about Europe's willingness to share the burden of security in our region.

Overseas Territories

15.   There are at present no immediate threats to these Territories. We must, however, be able to react to any emerging security problem and where necessary to assist the civil authorities.

Outside Europe

16.   Outside Europe, our interests are most directly affected by events in the Gulf and the Mediterranean, and we have bilateral understandings with some Gulf States which carry the strong expectation of military support. Risks in these areas are likely to grow rather than decline. This does not, of course, mean that we need to recreate a standing or permanent military capability "east of Suez". Elsewhere the risks to our interests are either small or we have more choice over the level of our response, which would be generally in combination with others.

17.   At the same time our planning needs to address new challenges: weapons proliferation, ethnic tensions, population pressures, environmental degradation, drugs, terrorism, crime and the failure of state structures.

18.   These new sources of conflict can have a direct impact in Britain. Over 90% of the heroin on our streets comes from Afghanistan, where the civil war makes it impossible to tackle the problem at its source. In an increasingly interdependent world, such global problems can undermine the international structures on which we and others depend. With Britain's unusually wide overseas interests and assets, including the ten million British citizens overseas, we are particularly vulnerable. The number of such conflicts is increasing. In its first four decades the UN authorised 18 peace-keeping missions; in the past decade it has authorised a further 25.

19.   We cannot turn our backs on the human suffering and economic and social damage which such crises cause. Our international stature and influence gives us a responsibility as well as an interest in responding to them. Our forces have a range of skills and capabilities which are particularly valuable in this context. Our primary means of tackling these problems are through preventive diplomacy and economic, social and developmental co-operation. However, military force, including its deterrent effect, can have a significant role to play when other forms of conflict prevention have failed.

20.   There will be more calls on our Armed Forces to become involved in averting, managing or countering these new security challenges, with other NATO Allies or other countries. We should retain the ability to become involved when it is in our interest to do so and it will be important to have clear objectives, criteria for success and an exit strategy.

21.   Our forces also make an important, often unsung, contribution to the spread of stability and democratic values through training and other forms of military assistance (now known as Defence Diplomacy); and through anti-drug operations at home and abroad.

22.   Our own interests require the international community as a whole to support and contribute to actions to ensure international security. To encourage others to help shoulder the burden, Britain should take on a share reflecting the spread of our interests and our political leadership role, particularly in the UN Security Council.

The Defence Contribution

23.   The Armed Forces make a major contribution to Britain's objectives in this rapidly changing world. They must not only be able to carry out the range of tasks which may arise from current priorities but also be sufficiently robust and flexible to cope with the longer term, when circumstances and priorities may change.

24.   Our analysis has shown that to do this, our force structures and military capabilities need to be based on:

–   ensuring European and therefore British security through a commensurate national contribution to the maintenance of NATO as a politically and militarily effective Alliance. This will include maintenance of nuclear deterrent forces (while pressing for multilateral negotiations towards mutual, balanced and verifiable reductions in nuclear weapons) and the ability to make an appropriate contribution to a regional conflict in Europe involving our NATO obligations, and retaining a framework on which it would be possible to rebuild over the longer term to meet a greater threat should one begin to emerge;

–   keeping the ability to respond, in combination with others, to threats to our important interests, in the Gulf and the Mediterranean. At the upper end of risks this could require capabilities which are similar in scale and nature to those which would be required for a regional conflict involving NATO;

–   providing support to the civil power in meeting internal security challenges in the United Kingdom and the Overseas Territories;

–   responding to lesser risks to British interests beyond these areas and to other direct calls on our forces, including any threats to Overseas Territories, assistance to British nationals overseas, and support to wider British interests at home and abroad. In responding to many of these risks, we would normally seek to operate in conjunction with others. We would not expect to maintain additional forces or capabilities specifically for these purposes;

–   supporting the Government's wider international responsibilities, including as a Permanent Member of the UN Security Council, particularly in relation to the maintenance of peace, international order and stability, humanitarian principles and democratic rights. Tasks of this sort are likely to be increasingly important, and may require a demanding range and scale of capabilities, although participation in individual operations will generally be a matter of choice;

–   helping to counter the risks from emerging global security problems such as proliferation, terrorism and international crime.

25.   Our vital stake in European security, our very important interests in the surrounding regions and our wider international responsibilities could each involve us in modern, high intensity conventional warfare. In all these cases, we could face opponents equipped with powerful modern equipment because of the increasing proliferation of weapons and technology. We therefore need forces which are flexible, highly capable, mobile and responsive. Recent experience has also shown us that our wider international responsibilities are now involving us in peace support operations where success depends on deterring or out-matching indigenous forces. This again requires forces trained and equipped for demanding conventional warfare.

26.   The work summarised in this essay formed the basis for subsequent stages of the Strategic Defence Review. We believe that all measures in the Review package are consistent with its conclusions.

SUPPORTING ESSAY THREE
THE IMPACT OF TECHNOLOGY

1. Technology and its application has been a high priority of the Strategic Defence Review, underpinning the themes of high capability forces and better value for money in defence. This essay looks at how, at a time of accelerating technological change, we can best take account of the impact of technology for defence purposes.

2. We need battle-winning forces to underpin our foreign and security policy. They must be able to make a distinctive, high quality contribution to multinational operations; and their equipment must give them a decisive technological edge over any potential opponent. If our forces are to remain contributors of quality to NATO and other multinational operations, our capabilities must be firmly at the high end of the technological spectrum and technically compatible with those of our allies. We must therefore ensure that we procure equipment based on high but proven technology.

3. Our Armed Forces must be able to conduct a wide range of operations, from high-intensity combat to peacekeeping. The MOD must also contribute towards the Government's wider objectives of building Britain's reputation in the international community, developing a skilled and well-educated workforce and providing opportunities for high technology work for British industries.

4. As scientific discovery and technological advance continue apace, so the military options available to potential aggressors increase. The military advantage will rest with those who most effectively identify and exploit battle-winning technology. This places a premium on the ability to generate and identify opportunities; adopt them for military use; and integrate them rapidly into platforms, weapons systems and force structures. Britain must therefore maintain an agile and effective research and development process.

5. It is the very pace of technological advance and the associated explosion of opportunities which makes it unlikely that every opportunity can be exploited. Hard choices will be required to cope with the wide range of possibilities within a limited budget. We must therefore focus on areas where we can really make a difference, such as communications and information systems, improved explosives, better sensors and improved simulation.

Changing Technology

The Pace of Change

6. Military planners have sometimes been slow to recognise, and the procurement process slow to exploit, the opportunities offered by advances in technology. With the accelerating pace of change we shall need to be especially alert to this issue. Moreover, whereas advances in science and technology for military purposes have historically had applications in the civil market, new advances in the civil market are increasingly having profound implications for our future military capability.

7. In electronics, software and information technology generally, civil investment in research and development is ten times greater than defence investment. The computing power of state-of-the-art systems is doubling every 18 months or so; this implies around a 100-fold increase over ten years. The impact of these developments will be all-pervasive because of their use in the vast majority of modern military systems. We have to accept that in these areas it is difficult to predict where technological advances may lead for more than about five years in the future. Nevertheless, the Smart Procurement initiative will ensure that fast moving technologies can be quickly developed to maintain the capability of in-service platforms and systems through technology insertion, thereby guarding against obsolescence.

8. If we are to meet our foreign and security policy objectives, we must also be able to operate on terms of broad technological parity within multinational operations, most probably involving the United States, and to counter opponents exploiting freely available civil technologies. Although we may be forced to replace or upgrade systems

dependent on fast-moving technology (weapons, sensors and communication equipment) more frequently than in the past, platforms are likely to retain their operational edge for longer because the technologies on which they depend (materials, structures and propulsion) will probably advance less rapidly, and because they will be designed to accommodate updates. Thus the balance of investment will shift from platforms in favour of the progressive update of in-service equipment.

The Revolution in Military Affairs

9.   The biggest change in the conduct of future military operations is likely to come not from the weapons alone but from the application of information technology to military command and control . There is a growing body of opinion, particularly in the US, that we are approaching a 'Revolution in Military Affairs' in which we will see a step change in military capabilities resulting from the synergistic combination of long-range precision weapons with networks of advanced sensors and data processors. Radically improved capabilities in the field of information processing and communications systems will increase situational awareness (knowing where hostile and friendly forces are, and where they are not) by combining information from all available sources and rapidly distributing it to those who need it, thus permitting more effective and efficient use of our forces. Smart long-range precision weapons will enable us to attack targets accurately from distance, thereby reducing our own and civilian casualties.

10.   Leaving aside the academic debate on whether or not a revolution is underway, it is clear that exploiting these technologies will lead to significant improvements in military capability. They will inevitably be led by the US. If Britain and other Allies can successfully tap into these developments, the result will be more effective coalition operations. Conversely, there is potential for multinational operations to become more difficult if compatible capabilities are not preserved. This could lead to political as well as military problems. Our priority must therefore be to ensure that we maintain the ability to make a high quality contribution to multinational operations and to operate closely with US forces throughout the spectrum of potential operations. To do this we may need to be selective about the technologies we develop nationally or on a European basis, and be prepared to use US technologies in other areas in order to continue to make a leading contribution to multinational operations.

11.   Keeping pace with the US is not solely dependent on funding. We are already talking to the US Administration about the policy implications. In parallel we will need to ensure that doctrine is developed to take full advantage of the potential of developing technologies.

12.   Our forward equipment programme contains a range of projects which will exploit key technologies. These include the airborne stand-off radar (ASTOR) surveillance system; and our indirect fire precision attack programme which will provide a range of smart, long-range, guided weapons delivered by rockets or extended range artillery. Long-range airborne systems include the Brimstone, Storm Shadow and Hellfire missiles. In addition, our Joint Battlespace Digitisation initiative is fundamental to our future defence capability. This initiative aims to improve operational effectiveness by integrating weapons platforms, sensors and command, control, intelligence and information systems. It takes account of current work in the same field by the US and other NATO Allies to ensure that the communication and information systems crucial for future multinational operations will be compatible. The programme also reflects the perception that by 2015, military operations will no longer be characterised as sea, land or air, but will merge into a single battlespace in which the ability to conduct joint and combined operations will be fundamental.

13.   The increasing dependence on high technology to ensure that our forces maintain the ability to fight and win when called upon may encourage some potential adversaries to adopt alternative weapons or unconventional strategies ('asymmetric warfare'). Our future plans will need to guard against introducing new weaknesses which aggressors could exploit and ensure that we have the capability to combat or defend against alternative weapon systems.

Human Factors

14.   The design of defence systems must take account of the capabilities and limitations of the people who will operate them. The principle underlying the application of technology in this area is to build on human strengths and mitigate human weaknesses. Development of improved detection, countermeasures and treatments for victims of increasing threats, such as chemical and biological warfare, is being addressed. There will also be a continuing need to provide lightweight protection against explosive blast and fragments, as well as against environmental extremes such as heat, cold and vibration.

15.   New equipment is also changing the role of people in battle. Technology offers the potential for reducing the exposure of personnel to situations of greatest risk, for example by allowing unmanned platforms to carry out roles previously requiring manned solutions. The most likely early application is in the use of unmanned aerial vehicles for reconnaissance. Our Phoenix programme is an important step, and we are committed to investigating the potential for their wider application. Other examples are the use of remote controlled unmanned vehicles for land and sea mine clearance, and the increased use of stand-off weapons. The increased automation of tasks can, however, isolate personnel from each other and from direct contact with the battle and potentially reduce their situational awareness. These issues must be understood and taken into account by such programmes as Joint Battlespace Digitisation.

Information Vulnerability

16.   Greater integration of information systems has major benefits, but it also introduces new risks and offers new opportunities for an adversary to attack our information networks, thus degrading the fighting effectiveness of our forces. We will continue to invest in high quality research and development to ensure that we are at the forefront of this technological challenge.

17.   The threat to information infrastructures is not just a defence issue. We are therefore working with other areas of Government, our allies and suppliers of key services to ensure that security policies and technical solutions match the developing nature of the infrastructure. We will provide appropriate resources to improve our ability to protect defence information networks, to deter those who would attack them and to provide an immediate warning of attack in order to counter and recover from such attacks. We will vigorously test these arrangements, make changes to policies and procedures where necessary, and provide training and education to assure the security and availability of information vital to the conduct of defence.

Modelling and Simulation

18.   Increasingly sophisticated and accurate computer modelling techniques are transforming systems development and training. They are reducing development time and cost by cutting the number of prototypes required, and improving the efficiency and effectiveness of designs. Advanced simulation also allows the computer-based representation of complex equipment and scenarios for operational and tactical training, and provides mission rehearsal and decision-making tools. This has the added advantages of reducing the number of expensive munitions expended in training, the wear on warfighting equipment and the use of training areas, and could eventually lead to a requirement for fewer items of equipment.

Reliability

19.   Civil equipment has become significantly more reliable in recent years, chiefly as a result of better manufacturing methods based on quality management and systems engineering. Our aim is to harness civilian best practice and apply it to military equipment. More reliable systems, which are easier to maintain and sustain in the field, will lead to a greater proportion available for operations at any one time. This too should mean that we can reduce the total number of systems required.

The MOD Response

20.   In its Manifesto, the Government pledged to nurture investment in new technologies. As part of this process, the Strategic Defence Review has re-examined and confirmed the importance of technology in defence.

21.   Excellence in specialised military fields, such as stealth, sensors, electronic warfare and guided weapons, will be essential, but there will also need to be closer links with the areas of civil technology described earlier. MOD will need to fund research aimed at incorporating the best of civil technology into military systems. Dual use (civil and military) research, in collaboration with industry, will be an important theme, as will increased international research collaboration.

Technology Strategy

22.   The MOD, in discussion with industry, has produced a formal technology strategy, first published in May 1996, aimed at maximising access to the science and technology that is available worldwide. The intention is to develop the MOD technology base in those areas most likely to enhance defence capability. The strategy guides the formulation, in consultation with the Defence Evaluation and Research Agency (DERA), of a research programme designed to close the gap between the capabilities provided by the existing technology base and those required in the future. Our objectives are:

- to ensure that MOD has access to impartial high quality technical advice so that it can act as an 'intelligent customer' and obtain value for money in procuring higher technology equipment;

- to enhance the ability of industry to respond cost-effectively to MOD's equipment requirements;

- to facilitate collaboration and research planning with industry, other Government departments and Allies; and,

- consistent with defence aims, to contribute to Britain's overall prosperity.

23.   The technology strategy provides a stable basis for the longer term planning of MOD's research programme, thus enabling other Government departments, industry and others to make plans accordingly. The strategy will, however, be updated at intervals in the light of changes to the military threat, technological opportunity and the views of stakeholders.

Technology Transfer

24.   The MOD makes an important contribution to technology transfer to industry. Each year we spend over £2Bn on defence equipment development, including some £450M on research with the DERA. Technology transfer is, of course, a two-way street and the MOD also benefits from industrial developments in the world market. It is these mutually beneficial processes which we would like to enhance.

25.   The Government's Manifesto said "we support a strong UK defence industry, which is a strategic part of our industrial base as well as our defence effort". In furtherance of this pledge, the Defence Secretary has re-invigorated the National Defence Industries Council, of which he is Chairman. One of the actions being taken forward under the Council's auspices is the preparation of a wider national technology strategy.

Defence Diversification

26. The main goal of technology transfer to civil industry is to accelerate and widen the diffusion of defence originated technology and techniques into the broader economy. This is easier said than done, and several reports produced by the Defence and Aerospace Panel of the Technology Foresight Programme have emphasised the need for better harmonisation of technical priorities between government, industry and academia.

27. We therefore see considerable value in fostering dialogue and networking amongst the Government, industrial and academic communities that formulate and deliver research programmes. Part of the expertise thus generated can be extended to civilian use more efficiently than at present, and we published our proposals for doing so in March 1998, in the consultative Green Paper *"Defence Diversification – Getting The Most Out Of Defence Technology"* (Cm 3861). The centrepiece of these proposals is to set up a Defence Diversification Agency.

28. The Agency would provide a focus for information on what is available, stimulate access to Government expertise and facilities, and encourage collaboration. It would also provide a confidential database of future defence needs, to enable companies to consider how their technology could be applied to defence, or to target research and development to meet known future markets. We believe that this will help to strengthen the technology and manufacturing base, thereby securing the capacity to provide our future equipment needs, and to sustain manufacturing output and employment in accordance with the Government's broader objectives.

International Collaboration

29. International operations have become the norm, and the Armed Forces regularly train alongside our allies to hone their interoperability. It clearly makes sense to have consensus on what the key technologies of the future are and how interoperability will be maintained. MOD intends to ensure that such a consensus exists by maintaining the strong international links between both military and policy making staffs. To stimulate debate both within Britain and internationally, we intend to publish periodic reports on how emerging technologies worldwide could affect future military operations.

30. International collaboration offers access to the 95% of scientific research conducted overseas. Collaborative research, currently involving more than 20 countries, is an essential part of our technology strategy. It contributes to both the breadth and quality of the MOD technology base, improves the value for money obtained from defence research, leads to greater commonality in operational requirements and helps to achieve improved interoperability with our allies. Britain has a great deal to offer, with world-class technology and expertise in a number of fields, such as in the detection of biological warfare agents and in avionics systems. We can use this expertise to trade with other countries to our mutual advantage. Our strategy includes the identification and establishment of new collaborative projects with nations who possess a capability in those areas of advanced technology rates as a key for our future defence needs. With this aim in mind, it is our intention to maintain or increase our collaborative research activities.

Technology Demonstration

31. Technology demonstration is intended to reduce technical risk inherent in high-technology projects and to encourage the transfer to industry of technology derived from defence research. We intend to increase the use of technology demonstration and to involve the military user at an early stage in the evaluation of new systems, drawing on the lesson of the successful US model of advanced concept technology demonstrators.

Conclusion

32.   One of the main lessons we have learned from our work on technology in the Strategic Defence Review is that in the future we will need to consider technology issues from a politico-military as well as a technical perspective. No country can hope to grasp every possible opportunity, but we have put in place the machinery to ensure that technology can be harnessed effectively for the Armed Forces. Our policy is to be able to make a distinctive, high quality contribution to multinational operations with equipment that is interoperable with our most advanced allies and has a decisive technological edge over our opponents. This presents a robust and ambitious goal for our use of technology which is given direction by a focused and coherent technology strategy.

SUPPORTING ESSAY FOUR
DEFENCE DIPLOMACY

1.   Defence diplomacy is not a new idea. Britain's Armed Forces have a proud record of providing support to peacetime diplomacy. Ship visits, exchanges with other countries' forces and the training of foreign personnel are a long established part of daily military business. Since the end of the Cold War, all three Services and MOD civil servants have made an important contribution to improving relations with former adversaries in Europe and in promoting stability worldwide. They have built schools in Bosnia, helped feed refugees in Africa, monitored arms control agreements and conducted major exercises with Poland and the Ukraine.

2.   In today's strategic environment, there is scope for doing much more. We must of course be able to deal effectively with crisis and conflict when it occurs. Equally important, however, is helping to prevent conflicts occurring in the first place. There is growing recognition internationally that bolder steps are required to forestall escalation into conflict, as reflected in the recent reports by Lord Carrington and the US Carnegie Commission. The Defence Secretary has described the contribution that Armed Forces can make to this process as 'defence diplomacy', and he has characterised its aim as disarmament of the mind.

A New Mission

3.   To give new impetus to these activities and signal that they are now an important priority for defence, it has been decided to make Defence Diplomacy one of the eight core Missions which define the activities which we expect our Armed Forces to be able to undertake. This will ensure that defence diplomacy is properly linked to policy objectives.

> We have defined the Defence Diplomacy Mission as follows:
>
> To provide forces to meet the varied activities undertaken by the MOD to dispel hostility, build and maintain trust and assist in the development of democratically accountable armed forces, thereby making a significant contribution to conflict prevention and resolution.

4.   Three specific Military Tasks will contribute most directly to this new Mission:

– arms control, non-proliferation, and confidence and security building measures;

– Outreach, a new Military Task, designed to contribute to security and stability in Central and Eastern Europe, particularly Russia, but also extending as far as countries in the Trans-Caucasus and Central Asia, through bilateral assistance and co-operation with the countries concerned;

– other defence diplomacy activities, covering those military assistance activities with overseas military forces and defence communities not covered under Outreach.

Arms control, non-proliferation, and confidence and security building measures are addressed in the following essay.

Outreach – Building Bridges in Europe

5.   Tension and conflict from Chechnya to Bosnia, and now in Kosovo, demonstrate that security and stability in Europe cannot be taken for granted. Britain's security depends ultimately on a secure and stable Europe. It is therefore in our interests that we remain actively committed to promoting peace and security throughout the continent.

6.   The MOD's Outreach programme of bilateral defence assistance complements NATO's work to help promote a safer, more stable Europe. Britain will make a major contribution to NATO's initiatives. We will:

   –   continue to provide assistance to Poland, Hungary and the Czech Republic to ensure they are effectively and efficiently integrated into NATO's military structure;

   –   work hard, within NATO and outside, to ensure that those countries that are not NATO members do not feel isolated. We will place particular emphasis on improving our already close bilateral defence relationships with Russia and Ukraine;

   –   take a full part in NATO's Euro-Atlantic Partnership Council to develop political consultation and the Partnership for Peace programme which provides for military co-operation with NATO's 28 Partner nations. During September this year, Britain will host a major Partnership for Peace exercise – Exercise CO-OPERATIVE BEAR 98 – which will allow NATO and Partner nations to develop further interoperability in the air delivery of humanitarian aid and aeromedical evacuation.

7.   There is no single way to achieve our objectives, individually or in concert with Allies. It requires the patient implementation of a variety of activities. Our national programme of Outreach will include:

   –   increased English language training to help our Partners work with us and in NATO;

   –   more high level visits, between senior MOD civil servants and military officers so that key decision makers are better able to understand each other;

   –   expert advice to Partners to accelerate the development of democratically accountable, cost effective armed forces;

   –   more opportunities for British troops to train with their counterparts in Central and Eastern Europe to build trust by fostering personal contacts at all levels;

   –   enhanced assistance in the field of military education through additional places at military schools and colleges, the provision of advice on defence management, military training, and the attachment of in-country advisers.

8.   Additional resources will be made available and targeted to ensure that they contribute in practical ways to ensuring security and stability in Europe.

Other Defence Diplomacy Activities

9.   Beyond Central and Eastern Europe, we have traditionally provided military assistance to friendly Governments in support of our defence and foreign policy objectives. The Defence Diplomacy initiative has given a new emphasis to these activities and reinforced the need to target our efforts carefully where they are really needed, and in ways which reinforce our interests and responsibilities in the widest sense.

10.   As with the Outreach programme, a range of activities supports this military task. They include:

   –   the provision of advice and training overseas through short term training teams, such as that provided to the Zimbabwe Defence Force on wilderness search and rescue and casualty evacuation techniques;

   –   the provision of loan service personnel, on longer periods of secondment, such as those currently assisting with the establishment of the Kuwaiti and Bangladeshi National Defence Colleges, and the team in South Africa which has assisted since 1994 with the integration of the then-existing armed forces (both statutory and non-statutory) into a new National Defence Force;

   –   training and education courses in Britain, where our aim is to build on our already excellent reputation;

– exercises with the armed forces of friendly countries, which help to develop regional stability and improve interoperability. Recent exercises with the Regional Security System in the Caribbean are a good example;

– establishment of a Defence Diplomacy Scholarship for overseas officers and officials;

– visits to friendly countries, which help maintain and develop friendly relations at all levels. These visits are usually scheduled additions to other operational activities.

Organising Defence Diplomacy

11. In-country representation is vital to the success of many aspects of defence diplomacy. This is provided by attaché, liaison and exchange posts. These individuals have the opportunity to develop strong bilateral relationships. Attachés in particular play a fundamental role in defence diplomacy and can ensure that the UK is aware of their host countries' interests and concerns.

12. Because of the nature and complexity of defence diplomacy, its aims will only be met by integrating the MOD's activities very closely with those of other Government Departments, particularly the Foreign and Commonwealth Office and the Department for International Development. We will, for example, be working with the Foreign and Commonwealth Office to ensure that we have the right number of attachés in the right places to meet our defence and security goals.

13. More generally, all those involved in defence will have a role to play as ambassadors for peace and security worldwide. This will require new skills and a shift in thinking. To help achieve this we will provide appropriate training to meet the requirements of defence diplomacy.

14. Finally, because this is in large part new territory, and we need to keep track of the impact of what we and others are doing, we will develop, with outside assistance, transparent methods for monitoring and evaluating security reform in those countries in which we invest the most. This will help us to prioritise assistance and to assess the relative merits of our activities.

Conclusion

15. The new emphasis on defence diplomacy will provide important support for Britain's foreign and security policy objectives, using defence resources in constructive and imaginative ways. This will put Britain in a strong position to make a real contribution to conflict prevention. Defence diplomacy is therefore a significant challenge for all involved in defence in the modern world.

SUPPORTING ESSAY FIVE
DETERRENCE, ARMS CONTROL AND PROLIFERATION

1.　　Deterrence, arms control and proliferation are critically important to Britain's security. All three issues have inspired sometimes heated public debate, and they have been the subject of many of the submissions made to the Strategic Defence Review and a major focus of the Review itself. Because of the priority the Government attaches to arms control and non-proliferation, they have been a key part of the Defence Diplomacy initiative described in the previous essay.

Deterrence

2.　　All of Britain's military capabilities have a role to play in preventing war. The possession of robust military forces, in conjunction with those of our Allies, presents potential adversaries with the prospect of losses outweighing any gains they might hope to make from aggression. Both nuclear and conventional forces therefore contribute to deterrence, providing a credible range of options for responding proportionately to an aggressor's behaviour.

3.　　But nuclear deterrence remains a controversial and complex issue because of the terrible consequences of any use of nuclear weapons. There are no easy answers here. The world would be a better place if such weapons were not still necessary, but the conditions for complete nuclear disarmament do not yet exist.

4.　　Progress has been made through the Strategic Arms Reduction Treaty process in reducing Russian and United States strategic range nuclear forces and deployed warheads. Nonetheless, very large numbers of strategic and shorter range nuclear weapons, and substantial conventional military capabilities, remain as a potent potential threat to the security of Britain and our Allies should current circumstances change for the worse. We and NATO have radically reduced our reliance on nuclear weapons, but in present conditions nuclear deterrence still has an important contribution to make in insuring against the re-emergence of major strategic military threats, in preventing nuclear coercion, and in preserving peace and stability in Europe.

5.　　The Government's General Election Manifesto therefore promised to retain Trident as the ultimate guarantee of the United Kingdom's security while pressing for multilateral negotiations towards mutual, balanced and verifiable reductions in nuclear weapons. When we are satisfied with progress towards our goal of the global elimination of nuclear weapons, we will ensure that British nuclear weapons are included in negotiations.

Britain's Nuclear Capability

6.　　Against this background, we have undertaken a fundamental re-examination of all aspects of Britain's nuclear posture. Three Trident submarines are already in service. The fourth and last, VENGEANCE, will be launched later this year and will enter service around the turn of the century. This fleet of four submarines will enable us to maintain continuous deterrent patrols over the lifetime of the Trident force.

Nuclear Force Reductions

7.　　Circumstances have, however, changed dramatically since Trident was ordered. The improvements in the strategic landscape have clearly reduced the nuclear deterrent capability we need to underpin our security.

8.   Reductions have already been made in our nuclear forces. Since 1992, the United Kingdom has given up:

  – the nuclear Lance missile and artillery roles we undertook previously with US nuclear weapons held under dual-key arrangements;

  – our maritime tactical nuclear capability, so that Royal Navy surface ships no longer have any capability to carry or deploy nuclear weapons;

  – all of our air-launched nuclear weapons.

Trident is now Britain's only nuclear system. We are the only nuclear power that has so far been prepared to take such an important step on the route to nuclear disarmament.

Warhead Numbers

9.   The reductions described above are very significant. But the Strategic Defence Review has concluded that in the improved strategic environment we can now go further. We have decided that:

  – we will maintain fewer than 200 operationally available nuclear warheads, a reduction of one third from the previous government's plans;

  – Trident submarines on deterrent patrol will carry 48 warheads. This is the same number as carried on our Polaris submarines when they entered service. It compares with the previous government's ceiling of 96 warheads on each submarine.

  – we have no operational need for any more than the 58 Trident missile bodies already delivered or on order.

10.   At the end of the Cold War, our nuclear forces comprised Chevaline warheads on Polaris missiles and several hundred WE177 free-fall bombs in the sub-strategic role. In future:

  – we will have only half the number of operationally available nuclear weapons, with less than 30% of the explosive power;

  – the 48 warheads deployed on each Trident submarine to meet both our strategic and sub-strategic requirements will have an explosive power one third less than the 32 Chevaline warheads which were eventually deployed on each Polaris submarine.

Details of the reductions in the size of our total stockpile and in the numbers of operationally available weapons are shown in *FIGURE 1*.

11.   A comparison of the United Kingdom's holdings of operational warheads with those of the other four Nuclear Weapon States is shown in *FIGURE 2* on page 5–4.

Nuclear Operational Posture.

12.   The new strategic environment also enables us to maintain our nuclear forces at reduced readiness:

  – only one Trident submarine is on deterrent patrol at any time;

  – the submarines are routinely at a "notice to fire" measured in days rather than the few minutes' quick reaction alert sustained throughout the Cold War. Their missiles are de-targeted;

  – submarines on patrol will carry out a variety of secondary tasks, without compromising their security, including hydrographic data collection, equipment trials and exercises with other vessels;

  – over time we plan to reduce from double to single crews for each submarine, reflecting reduced operational tempo.

United Kingdom Nuclear Stockpile data — Figure 1

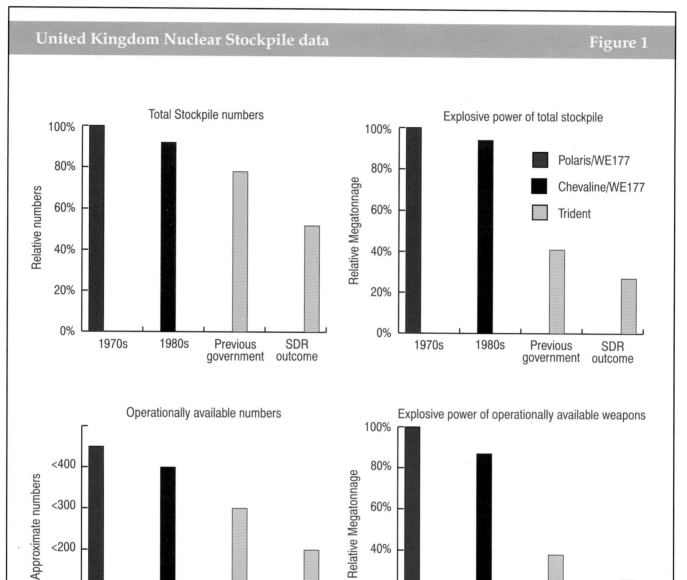

NOTES

1.   The charts compare our nuclear weapon holdings during the 1970s and 1980s with the previous government's plans for British nuclear forces by the end of 1999 and SDR decisions. The charts do not include United States' systems formerly operated by Britain under dual key arrangements.

2.   The figures for total stockpile numbers include all British nuclear weapons, excluding only weapons, such as WE177 and Chevaline, which have been withdrawn from service and are awaiting final dismantlement.

3.   The figures for operationally available numbers additionally exclude missile warheads held as a necessary processing margin or for technical surveillance purposes.

Figure 2

Nuclear Holdings of the Five Nuclear Weapon States (Warhead Numbers)

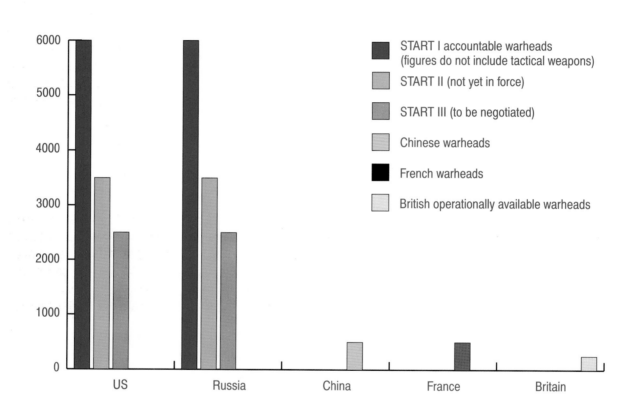

NOTES

1. Table covers the nuclear warhead holdings of the five Nuclear Weapon States, including Britain, under the Nuclear Non-Proliferation Treaty (NPT). Only India, Pakistan, Israel, Cuba and Brazil have not signed the NPT. Brazil has stated its intention to do so.

2. Holdings for the United States and Russia represent the limit on accountable strategic warheads set under START I (to be achieved by 2001), the upper limit set in START II (to be achieved by 2007 once the Treaty has entered into force) and the upper limit discussed by the US and Russia for a START III treaty. The United States additionally holds some stocks of non-strategic nuclear weapons and Russia has a stockpile of several thousand tactical nuclear weapons.

3. Holdings for China represent what is known about the total size of China's nuclear forces, including both strategic and tactical weapons.

4. Holdings for France represent all French nuclear forces, comprising submarine-launched ballistic missile warheads and air-launched weapons.

5. Holdings for Britain represent SDR decisions on numbers of operationally available Trident warheads to meet both the strategic and sub-strategic roles.

Other options considered in the Review

13.   During the Review, consideration was given to more radical de-alerting measures, such as taking submarines off deterrent patrol, and removing warheads from their missiles and storing them separately ashore. Some of the outside inputs to the Review suggested Britain should move in these or similar directions. Our work concluded, however, that neither step would be compatible in current circumstances with maintaining a credible minimum deterrent with a submarine-based nuclear system. Ending continuous deterrent patrols would create new risks of crisis escalation if it proved necessary to sail a Trident submarine in a period of rising tension or crisis. The further step of removing warheads from missiles would also add a new vulnerability to our deterrent posture. This is a particular concern given our reduction to a single nuclear system. It could force a government into earlier and hastier decision making if strategic circumstances were to deteriorate. Either step would undermine the stabilising role that Britain's nuclear deterrent forces would otherwise play in a developing crisis.

Atomic Weapons Establishment

14.   For as long as Britain has nuclear forces, we will ensure that we have a robust capability at the Atomic Weapons Establishment to underwrite the safety and reliability of our nuclear warheads, without recourse to nuclear testing. There are no current plans for any replacement for Trident, and no decision on any possible successor system would be needed for several years. But we have concluded that it would be premature to abandon a minimum capability to design and produce a successor to Trident should this prove necessary. However, the Government's aim is to take forward the process of nuclear disarmament to ensure that our security can in future be secured without nuclear weapons.

Nuclear Transparency

15.   Maintaining a degree of uncertainty about our precise capabilities is a necessary element of credible deterrence. Nonetheless, this Government is committed to being as open as possible about Britain's nuclear forces. The information we have now given about the number of warheads deployed on our Trident submarines and on aspects of previous systems such as our WE177 bombs, Polaris and Chevaline goes considerably further than previous governments. We will also be more open about stocks of fissile material; details are set out in paragraph 26.

Trident Acquisition Costs

16.   The principle of greater openness applies to the costs of nuclear forces. The current estimate of the total acquisition cost of the Trident programme is £12.52Bn. This figure (known as the non-hybrid estimate) covers all expenditure, including payments already made, at the price base and exchange rate assumed in the latest long term costing of the Defence programme. It represents a reduction in real terms of £177M from last year.

17.   The programme shows an overall reduction in costs, including the savings resulting from the decision to process missiles at the United States facility at Kings Bay, of some £3.7Bn compared with the original estimate. The vast majority of the costs of procuring Trident have now been spent. Expenditure on the Trident acquisition programme to the end of February 1998 represented some 91% of the estimate expressed in actual outturn prices. This is shown in *FIGURE 3*.

Estimate Table			Figure 3
	US £M	UK £M	Total £M
Previous estimate (March 1997) at 1996/97 economic conditions (£1=$1.5205)	3,645	8,925	12,570
Real changes	-67	-110	-177
Price Inflation	+76 (2.1%)	+262 (3%)	+338
Exchange Rate Variation between March 1997 and March 1998	-211	N/A	-211
Revised Estimate at 1997/98 economic conditions (£1=$1.6137)	3,443	9,077	12,520

NOTE

    Estimate does not include procurement costs of £167M for Spearfish torpedoes carried by Trident submarines.

Trident Operating Costs

18.   Within the Review, the operating costs of the Trident force have been re-examined to ensure that all the costs relevant to the support of Trident have been identified and to take into account recent operating experience. This has shown that the average annual operating cost of the Trident force over a planned thirty-year life is expected to be around £280M. Earlier estimates derived from a less rigorous exercise conducted in advance of actual operating experience. This figure does not represent the amount that would be saved by giving up our deterrent given the substantial transitional costs that would be involved. A breakdown of the operating costs is shown in *FIGURE 4*.

Nuclear Warhead Programme Costs

19.   The nuclear warhead programme costs directly related to Trident in financial year 1997/98 are estimated at £114M. Expenditure on our nuclear warhead programme as a whole amounted to £410M. This included the cost of decommissioning weapons withdrawn from service; substantial continuing costs arising from earlier stages of our

nuclear warhead programme; infrastructure costs at the Atomic Weapons Establishment (including expenditure to achieve safety and environmental improvements); and other activities, including support to other Government Departments and Comprehensive Test Ban Treaty verification. The overall cost of the warhead programme is declining. A breakdown of the costs is shown in *FIGURE 5* on page 5–8.

Estimate[1] for Direct Operating Costs of the Trident submarine force over its service life	Figure 4
Element	Annual Operating Costs, £million, averaged over 30 year life of Trident
Manpower[2]	33
In-Service Support of Submarine[3]	33
In-Service Support: Nuclear Propulsion	13
In-Service Support: Trident Missile System	47
Base/Site Running Costs	61
Refit-Maintenance	53
Stores and Spares	35
In-Service Trials	1
Dedicated Communications	1
Total	277

Notes:

1. This estimate has been derived from a compilation of 30-year estimates covering the activities listed above which are directly attributable to the operation of the Trident force. They are based on current assumptions about operating patterns. These estimates are shown as an annual average for presentational purposes only. They do not represent actual expenditure in a given year nor the amount which might be saved if the activity were terminated.

2. Includes: operational crews, specialist crew training, dedicated shore staff, and technical staff.

3. Includes: the command system, sonar, and Spearfish.

	Figure 5
Nuclear Warhead Programme: Estimated Expenditure in 1997/98 on current and earlier Nuclear-Warhead Related Activities	
	£million
Direct Trident Related Warhead Expenditure	
(a) *Trident Production costs at Atomic Weapons Establishment (AWE)*	*20*
(b) *Trident In-Service Support at AWE*	*9*
(c) *Research, Development and Capability Maintenance at AWE*	*58*
(d) *Trident related waste management at AWE*	*4*
(e) *Other warhead programme expenditure outside AWE*	*23*
Sub-Total	*114*
AWE Infrastructure	
(f) *Maintenance, safety and environmental improvements to meet Nuclear Installations Inspectorate requirements*	*168*
Other Activities	
(g) *Other activities including support to other Government Departments and Comprehensive Test Ban Treaty monitoring*	*19*
Costs Arising From Earlier Programmes	
(h) *Breakdown and dismantlement of WE177 and Chevaline warheads*	*11*
(i) *Payments to British Nuclear Fuels Limited and United Kingdom Atomic Energy Authority etc. in respect of liabilities from earlier stages of the UK nuclear programme*	*103*
(j) *Management and disposal of and waste at AWE from earlier stages of UK nuclear programme, and decommissioning of redundant facilities*	*13*
Sub-Total	*127*
Total	***428***
Less 1996/97 VAT receipt £18m	*–18*
GRAND TOTAL	***410***

NOTE

Total AWE running costs comprise all above elements excluding (e) and (i) to give a total of **£302M**.

Arms Control

20.   Consideration of how best to carry forward the Government's commitment to the elimination of nuclear weapons has been a key aspect of the Review. But this goal cannot be achieved in isolation from wider political and security realities, including the recent nuclear tests in India and Pakistan. The challenge is to create the conditions in which no state judges that it needs nuclear weapons to guarantee its security. The radical improvements in European security in recent years have shown that this is not an impossible objective. But it is not a task for the Nuclear Weapon States alone. All states have their part to play.

21.   The Government welcomes the continuing bilateral START process between the US and Russia, and looks forward to prompt Russian ratification of START II, to enable early negotiations on further bilateral reductions in their strategic holdings, under START III, as agreed by Presidents Clinton and Yeltsin at Helsinki in March 1997. In parallel, with our NATO Allies, we are consulting with Russia in the NATO-Russia Permanent Joint Council on issues relating to Russia's continuing substantial holdings of non-strategic nuclear weapons.

The Nuclear Non-Proliferation Treaty

22.   The Government is unequivocally committed to Britain's obligations under the Nuclear Non-Proliferation Treaty. The effective implementation of all its provisions is vital for global peace and security, and we attach great importance to the strengthened review process agreed in 1995. We also welcome the various measures taken by the International Atomic Energy Agency in recent years to strengthen its safeguards systems.

23.   We have to stop nuclear proliferation to reach our goal of a world free of nuclear weapons. There is a clear international consensus that the way to achieve this is through the Nuclear Non-Proliferation Treaty (NPT) and the Comprehensive Nuclear Test Ban Treaty (CTBT). By testing, India and Pakistan have challenged this consensus. They risk igniting a dangerous arms race and endangering stability in and beyond their region. This is the wrong way to go. We and many other states, including through a resolution by the UN Security Council, have called upon both countries to join the global regime against nuclear proliferation by signing the CTBT and joining in negotiations on a Fissile Material Cut-Off Treaty without conditions. We are seeking commitments that they will not weaponise or deploy nuclear weapons or missiles. Our goal continues to be the adherence by all states, including India and Pakistan, to the NPT as it stands. This treaty is the cornerstone of the international non-proliferation regime and the essential foundation for the pursuit of nuclear disarmament.

The Comprehensive Test Ban Treaty

24.   Britain ratified the Comprehensive Nuclear Test Ban Treaty on 6 April this year, alongside France. We were the first two Nuclear Weapon States to do so, and hope the others will soon follow; this is a prerequisite for the Treaty to enter into force. By ending nuclear testing the Treaty constrains the development of new types of nuclear weapons. It therefore represents an important step towards global disarmament. Britain played an important role in the Treaty negotiations, particularly in the design of the International Monitoring System to verify compliance. The Government is working for its effective establishment at the earliest practicable date. Britain is one of the few countries so far to have paid its contributions to it in full. We will also maintain our national monitoring and analysis capability.

A Fissile Material Cut-Off Treaty

25.   To complement the Comprehensive Test Ban Treaty, a key priority is a verifiable, legally binding convention banning the future production of fissile material for nuclear weapons or other nuclear explosive devices (a Fissile Material Cut-Off Treaty). This is an essential step towards global elimination of nuclear weapons, and the Government is prepared to enter into immediate negotiations for such a treaty in the Conference on Disarmament.

Fissile Material Management

26.   Britain is legally entitled to hold stocks of nuclear materials needed for national security outside international safeguards. As part of our commitment to the control of fissile material, the Government is now ready to be the first Nuclear Weapon State to declare the total size of these stocks. They comprise:

- – 7.6 tonnes of plutonium;

- – 21.9 tonnes of highly enriched uranium; and

- – 15,000 tonnes of other forms of uranium.

Much of this stock is no longer required for defence purposes, and 4.4 tonnes of plutonium, including 0.3 tonnes of weapons-grade plutonium, and over 9,000 tonnes of non-highly enriched uranium will now be placed under European Atomic Energy Community (EURATOM) safeguards, and made liable to inspection by the International Atomic Energy Agency (IAEA). All stocks of highly enriched uranium will, however, be retained outside safeguards, since material no longer needed for nuclear weapons will be used for the naval propulsion programme. We have considered whether further disaggregation of these totals at this time would be compatible with our continuing, if reduced, security requirement. We have concluded that it would not.

27.   All re-processing of spent fuel from defence reactors at Chapelcross will in future be conducted under EURATOM safeguards and made liable to inspection by the IAEA. This will mean that all planned future reprocessing and enrichment in the UK will take place under international safeguards. We will, however, retain the right to resume such activities outside safeguards until agreement is reached on a Fissile Material Cut-Off Treaty. Britain also has the right to withdraw material from safeguards for reasons of national security (including such purposes as radiography at defence nuclear facilities), but withdrawals will be limited to small quantities of materials not suitable for explosive purposes, and the details will be made public. Defence nuclear facilities will continue to remain outside international supervision.

28.   Eliminating nuclear weapons will require states which have had nuclear programmes outside international safeguards to account for fissile material produced. We will therefore begin a process of declassification and historical accounting with the aim of producing by Spring 2000 an initial report of defence fissile material production since the start of Britain's defence nuclear programme in the 1940s.

Nuclear Verification

29.   Verification of arms control and non-proliferation agreements is critical to their effectiveness, and has therefore been examined in the Review. It has traditionally been an issue on which Britain has made a substantial contribution. Over time we have developed particular expertise in the nuclear field in the monitoring of fissile materials, particularly through our involvement in the development of the IAEA's safeguards system, and in monitoring of nuclear tests. The Government intends to maintain these strengths, which will be important in implementing the Comprehensive Nuclear Test Ban Treaty and in negotiating a Fissile Material Cut-Off Treaty.

30.   But Britain has only a very limited capability at present to verify the reduction and elimination of nuclear weapons. A programme is therefore being set in hand to develop expertise in this area, drawing in particular on the skills of specialists at the Atomic Weapons Establishment. A small team will be established to consider technologies, skills and techniques, and to identify what is already available to us in the United Kingdom. The Government will consider how to take this programme forward in the light of the team's interim conclusions. The aim is to ensure that, when the time comes for the inclusion of British nuclear weapons in multilateral negotiations, we will have a significant national capability to contribute to the verification process.

Negative Security Assurances

31.   Britain has repeatedly made it clear that we will not use nuclear weapons against a non-nuclear weapon state not in material breach of its nuclear non-proliferation obligations, unless it attacks us, our Allies or a state to which we have a security commitment, in association or alliance with a nuclear weapon state. Britain has also undertaken to seek immediate UN Security Council action to assist any non-nuclear-weapon state party to the Non-Proliferation Treaty that is attacked or threatened with nuclear weapons. In addition, we would be prepared to take appropriate measures in response to a request from the victim for technical, medical, scientific or humanitarian assistance.

32.   We:

- welcome and support the recent re-establishment of an Ad Hoc Committee on Security Assurances at the Conference on Disarmament in Geneva;

- believe that the further extension of regional nuclear-weapon-free zones has an important role to play where the conditions are right;

- ratified the relevant protocols to the Treaty of Raratonga (South Pacific Nuclear Free Zone) in September 1997;

- intend to ratify the protocols to the Treaty of Pelindaba (African Nuclear-Weapon-Free Zone) soon;

- hope to be able to sign the protocol to the Treaty of Bangkok (South East Asian Nuclear-Weapon-Free Zone);

- support the initiative by the States of Central Asia to establish a nuclear-weapon-free zone in their region.

FIGURE 6 shows Nuclear-Weapon-Free Zones.

33.   In the modern world, nuclear weapons are not the only weapon of mass destruction. The Review therefore addressed the continuing risks arising from the proliferation of chemical and biological weapons. The Government is committed to their elimination. But the difficulty and complexity of this task should not be underestimated.

34.   The Government's policy has two main strands:

- existing international arms control and non-proliferation regimes must be strengthened, increasing the political and economic costs to proliferators, and the risk of their being detected by the international community;

- as long as risks remain, British forces must be trained and equipped to operate in a chemical or biological environment. This fulfils our duty of care to our people and, by ensuring that there is no military benefit from using chemical or biological weapons, it reduces the incentives for a proliferator to acquire them.

In the long term, we seek to create the conditions where no state can credibly judge that the gains from acquiring such weapons would be equal to the costs and risks involved.

Figure 6

Nuclear-Weapon-Free Zones

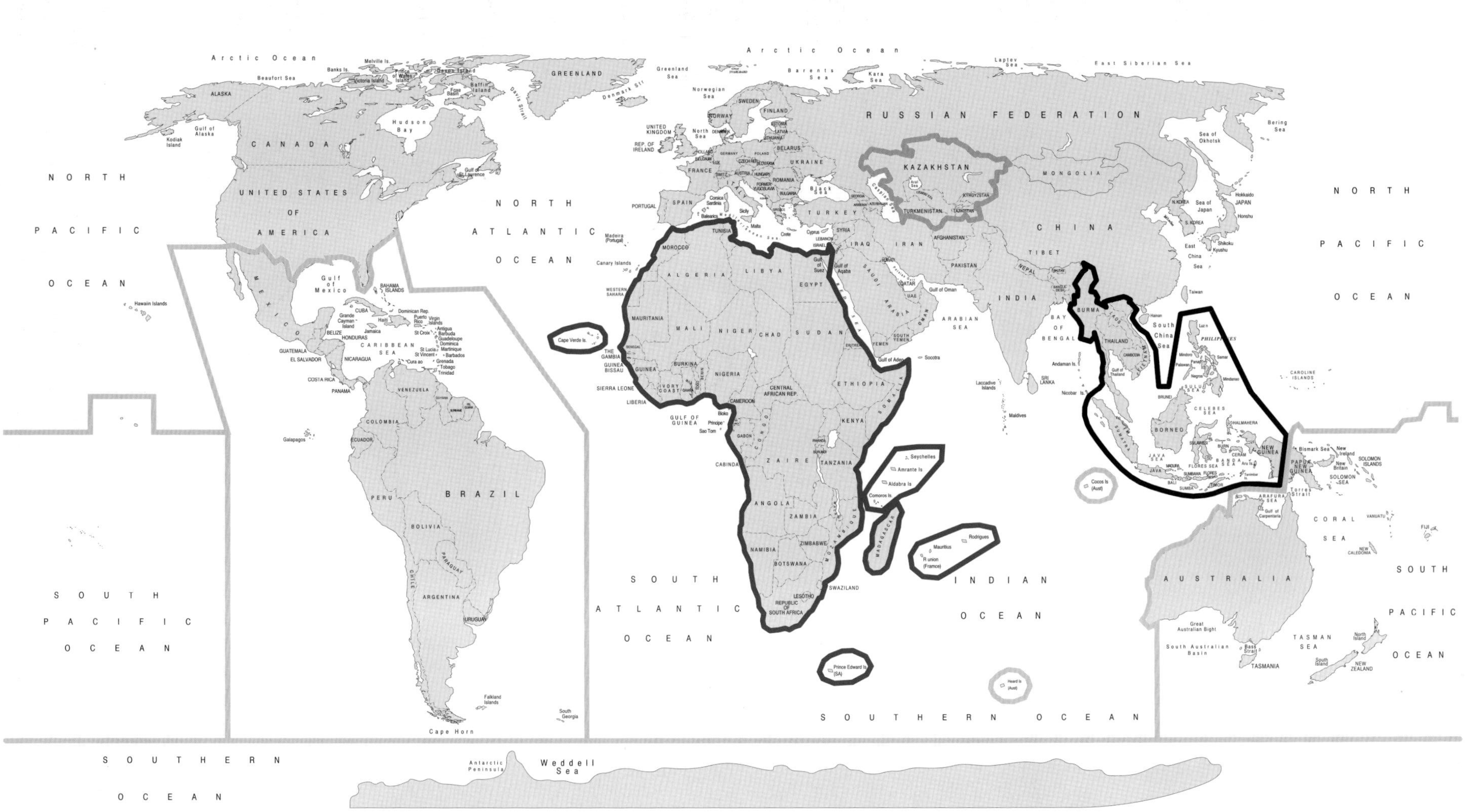

NWFZ in force; Recognised by the Nuclear Weapon States (NWS)

NWFZ in force; Not yet recognised by the NWS

NWFZ not yet in force; Recognised by the NWS

NWFZ Under negotiation

NOTE: Boundaries are not authoritative.

Chemical Weapons

35.   The Chemical Weapons Convention was opened for signature in 1993 and entered into force last year. It bans the development, production, stockpiling and use of chemical weapons, and requires the destruction of existing stockpiles. The Government is working closely with the international inspectorate – the Organisation for the Prohibition of Chemical Weapons (OPCW) – to ensure that the Treaty is implemented in full as soon as possible. The Chemical and Biological Defence sector at Porton Down has a programme to develop chemical and biological arms control technologies. We are also considering whether we can assist Russia in dismantling the vast stocks of chemical weapons it inherited from the Soviet Union.

36.   Implementation of the Chemical Weapons Convention in the United Kingdom is the responsibility of the Department of Trade and Industry. Britain was one of the first states to agree to have its relevant defence and industrial facilities inspected under the Convention, and all these inspections to date have been completed successfully. We are working with the OPCW in developing its inspection capabilities; in February this year, at our invitation, the OPCW conducted its first joint practice challenge inspection at RAF Valley in Anglesey.

Biological Weapons

37.   The Government also wants to strengthen the Biological and Toxin Weapons Convention (BTWC), which entered into force in 1975. It is now known that at least two states, the Soviet Union and Iraq, conducted illegal offensive programmes for many years after signing it. Since 1996 negotiations have been underway in Geneva on measures to strengthen the Convention.

38.   Britain is playing a major role in the BTWC negotiations and, during our Presidency, the European Union agreed a common position. This contains an undertaking to seek to conclude substantive negotiations this year, to allow an agreed Protocol to be adopted by the States Parties to the BTWC at a Special Conference early in 1999. It spells out four key elements which we believe must be in the Protocol:

- declarations of a range of facilities and activities of potential relevance under the Convention, so as to enhance transparency;

- provision for visits to facilities in order to promote accurate and complete declarations, and thus further enhance transparency and confidence;

- provision for rapid and effective investigations into concerns over non-compliance, including facility and field investigations;

- a cost-effective and independent organisation, including a small permanent staff, capable of implementing the Protocol effectively.

39.   Britain has firmly supported the efforts of the United Nations Special Commission on Iraq (UNSCOM) to identify and destroy Iraq's arsenal of chemical and biological weapons, along with its nuclear weapons programmes and its ballistic missile delivery systems, in accordance with Iraq's own undertakings to this effect. But Iraq's latest attempts to evade its commitments under numerous UN Security Council resolutions, and the Soviet Union's previous clandestine offensive biological weapons programme, have demonstrated how difficult it is to prevent a nation determined to ignore international norms and controls from acquiring chemical or biological weapons.

The risks from proliferation

40.   Our assessment is that there could be around 20 countries that either possess or have shown an interest in developing offensive chemical and/or biological warfare capabilities. The Government is also concerned about the nuclear programmes of some non-nuclear weapons states, as well as India and Pakistan. Proliferation is not simply a matter of weapons but of delivery systems as well. These include ballistic missiles, which may be used to deliver nuclear, biological or chemical weapons. At present, any risk to Britain from the ballistic missiles of nations of concern

in terms of proliferation is many years off, but the risk to some of our NATO allies is less distant; and British forces must be able to operate in regions, such as the Gulf, where they might face these risks.

Non-Proliferation and Export Controls

International Export Control Regimes					Figure 7
MEMBER COUNTRY	Australia Group (chemical and biological weapons)	Nuclear Suppliers Group (nuclear)	Zangger Commitee (nuclear)	Missile Technology Control Regime	Wassenaar Arrangement (conventional/ dual-use goods)
Argentina	●	◆	▲	■	○
Australia	●	◆	▲	■	○
Austria	●	◆	▲	■	○
Belgium	●	◆	▲	■	○
Brazil		◆		■	
Bulgaria		◆	▲		○
Canada	●	◆	▲	■	○
China			▲		
Czech Republic	●	◆	▲		○
Denmark	●	◆	▲	■	○
Finland	●	◆	▲	■	○
France	●	◆	▲	■	○
Germany	●	◆	▲	■	○
Greece	●	◆	▲	■	○
Hungary	●	◆	▲	■	○
Iceland	●			■	
Ireland	●	◆	▲	■	○
Italy	●	◆	▲	■	○
Japan	●	◆	▲	■	○
Latvia		◆			
Luxembourg	●	◆	▲	■	○
Netherlands	●	◆	▲	■	○
New Zealand	●	◆		■	○
Norway	●	◆	▲	■	○
Poland	●	◆	▲		○
Portugal	●	◆	▲	■	○
Romania	●	◆	▲		○
Russia		◆	▲	■	○
Slovakia	●	◆	▲	■	○
South Africa		◆	▲	■	
South Korea	●	◆	▲		○
Spain	●	◆	▲	■	○
Sweden	●	◆	▲	■	○
Switzerland	●	◆	▲	■	○
Turkey				■	○
Ukraine		◆	▲		○
United Kingdom	●	◆	▲	■	○
United States	●	◆	▲	■	○

NOTE: As at 30 June 1998.

41.   The Government strongly supports diplomatic measures to prevent the proliferation and development of chemical and biological weapons, and their means of delivery, and will continue to work actively to this end. Britain is a founding member of all the export control regimes (the Nuclear Suppliers Group, Zangger Committee, Australia Group, the Missile Technology Control Regime and the Wassenaar Arrangement) and we are committed to improving their effectiveness.

Defence Responses to Proliferation

42.   In addition to these measures, we need military capabilities to address the risks to British forces deployed overseas posed by nuclear, biological and chemical weapons and their means of delivery. To do otherwise would be an unacceptable constraint on our political freedom of action and could put our people at undue risk. Britain has played a pivotal role in NATO work in defining the capabilities needed to respond to these risks. The Strategic Defence Review addressed responses which might now be required at the national level.

43.   A crucial element is to ensure the fullest possible information on the intentions and capabilities of countries of concern. It is often difficult to establish the facts but we will continue to devote significant resources to this effort.

44.   There is no "silver bullet" which will provide a complete answer to the risks posed by chemical and biological weapons. What is needed is a balance of capabilities, to deter, counter, and defend against the use of such weapons. Protective measures will play an important part, including detection capabilities and the possibility of immunising personnel; so too will other conventional capabilities which can play a role in defeating key targets relating to the programmes of countries of concern.

Ballistic Missile Defence

45.   A number of systems intended to destroy ballistic missiles are under development, notably in the United States. These may play a role within a balanced spectrum of capabilities to counter the risks posed by chemical and biological weapons and their means of delivery. But technologies in this area are changing rapidly and it would, at this stage, be premature to decide on acquiring such a capability. We will, however, monitor developments in the risks posed by ballistic missiles and in the technology available to counter them, participate in NATO studies, and work closely with our Allies to inform future decisions.

Review of Defence Responses to Proliferation

46. The Strategic Defence Review has heightened awareness of the challenge British forces would face if they had to operate in a potentially hostile nuclear, biological or chemical environment and has identified various inherited shortfalls in Britain's defensive capabilities against these weapons. To address these shortfalls, we will:

- increase planned procurement of land-based biological detection equipments;
- establish a joint Army and Royal Air Force nuclear, biological and chemical defence capability, manned mostly by Regular personnel, available at high readiness to help protect deployed forces;
- continue to develop vaccines against known biological agents.

47.   These measures will help meet immediate problems. In the longer term, we intend to go further to ensure a coherent national response to these threats. A further detailed review, building on work undertaken in NATO, has been set in hand. Work should be completed by the Summer Recess. A summary of the resulting conclusions will then be made public.

Conventional Arms Control

48.   Conventional arms control has contributed very significantly to the overall lowering of tension in Europe. The Government is firmly committed, with our Allies and Partners, to proceed with this process. The main conventional arms control agreements involving the United Kingdom are the Conventional Armed Forces in Europe Treaty (CFE and CFE1A), the Vienna Document 94 and the Open Skies Treaty.

CFE Adaptation

49. The central challenge at present is to ensure the continuing relevance of the 1990 CFE Treaty. This limits the numbers of heavy weapons in the 30 countries of NATO and the former Warsaw Pact. Over 50,000 heavy weapons have now been destroyed or otherwise reduced since the Treaty was signed. But the Treaty was negotiated at the end of the Cold War, and now needs adapting to reflect changes in the European security environment. Negotiations between the 30 States Parties started in Vienna in January 1997, and are likely to last well into 1999. The Government is fully committed to their successful conclusion. As CFE is at the heart of co-operative European security, its adaptation is a fundamental part of NATO's developing relationship with Russia and other partners, and of the process of building security conditions in Europe which in time may allow us to dispense with nuclear weapons.

The Vienna Document and Open Skies

50.   In the same vein and a similar timescale, work is under way to revise the Vienna Document 94. This is a politically binding agreement by the 54 participating States of the Organisation for Security and Co-operation in Europe (OSCE), which promotes transparency, stability and openness in military affairs. Britain also continues to use contacts with Russia, Ukraine and Belarus to encourage their ratification of the 1992 Open Skies Treaty. When it enters into force, this will enhance other arms control agreements by providing for the over-flight and photography of participating States Parties' territory. To demonstrate that we are committed to putting principles into action, the Government will restore Britain's active contribution to Open Skies implementation by committing a specialised Andover aircraft to conduct photographic overflights, and encourage other states to undertake similar flights over Britain.

The Dayton Agreement

51.   Britain also actively supports the Dayton Arms Control process as a member of the Contact Group. We welcomed the OSCE decision last December to initiate consultations and negotiations on a new agreement to further enhance stability and security in the Balkans and the surrounding region. This will build on the successes of the current agreements under Dayton Articles II (confidence and security building measures) and IV (CFE-style reductions and limitations).

Humanitarian Obligations

52.   All States have an obligation to minimise and alleviate the consequences of conflict for innocent civilians. This is fundamental to an ethical security and defence policy, and we have clearly shown our commitment in this area, in particular by our efforts to ban anti-personnel landmines, and to ratify the Additional Protocols to the Geneva Convention.

Anti-personnel landmines

53. The Government has devoted much energy to the issue of anti-personnel landmines (APLs) since coming to office, and we were delighted to be among the first signatories of the Ottawa Convention on 3 December 1997. Our intention is to ratify the Convention as quickly as possible. In the meantime, work is well under way to fulfil our obligations under the Convention by, for example, a programme to destroy stockpiled operational APLs by 1 January 2000, well in advance of the agreed deadline. We have also considerably enhanced our activities in the area of humanitarian demining, for example by establishing a Mine Information and Training Centre at Minley, and by the gift of ten demining tractors to the HALO Trust.

Additional Protocols

54.   The United Kingdom signed but did not ratify the Additional Protocols to the 1949 Geneva Conventions in 1977. They further codify and develop the laws of armed conflict set out in the Geneva Conventions and Britain played a leading role in their negotiation. Additional Protocol I contains rules protecting the victims of international armed conflict, particularly women and children. Additional Protocol II governs internal armed conflict and provides fundamental guarantees of humane treatment for persons who do not take part or have ceased to take a direct part in hostilities. We regarded our ratification after 20 years as a matter of priority. The United Kingdom accordingly ratified on 28 January 1998.

Conclusion

55.   The Government is committed to the goal of the global elimination of nuclear, biological and chemical weapons. We will work to create conditions in which even a minimum level of nuclear deterrence is no longer necessary. Until then, Britain will maintain the minimum level of nuclear deterrent necessary to prevent the possibility of major war in Europe. At the same time, we will work to remove the risk of proliferation of nuclear, biological and chemical weapons worldwide, while maintaining a robust defensive capability to protect British interests in the event of their use. The Government is convinced that the interconnecting policies and programmes set out above, which have either emerged from or been confirmed by the analysis and conclusions of the Strategic Defence Review, represent a coherent, ethical and militarily sound contribution to British security.

SUPPORTING ESSAY SIX
FUTURE MILITARY CAPABILITIES

1.   The aim of the Strategic Defence Review has been to reshape and modernise Britain's Armed Forces for the 21st century. All three Services have undergone great changes in the last decade (see *FIGURE 1*). At the same time, military personnel and the civilians who support them have had to cope with high levels of operational activity which few would have predicted at the end of the Cold War.

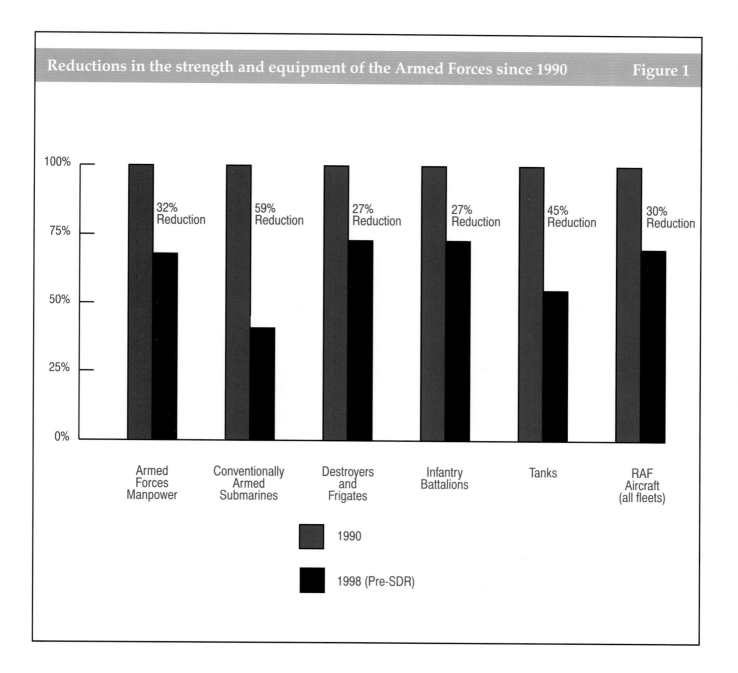

Reductions in the strength and equipment of the Armed Forces since 1990   **Figure 1**

2.   Nobody with an understanding of defence issues would argue that the Armed Forces should be immune to change. But changes to military capabilities must be matched to changes in the strategic environment, and to the activities we expect our forces to undertake. A process of evolution has been taking place throughout the last decade, and in some respects our forces are well prepared for the challenges of the next century. But the process is not yet complete. This essay explains how we have sought to ensure that Britain's Forces are the right size and shape, with the people they need for the tasks we want them to undertake.

I Process

3.   To translate the Review's policy framework into a detailed basis for determining Britain's defence needs, a comprehensive set of planning assumptions was developed. This methodology has been used before but it was refined and expanded considerably during the Review.

4.   The first step was to define the <u>Missions</u> which the Armed Forces must be able to undertake in support of foreign and security policy, and develop them into specific <u>Military Tasks</u>. The Missions are set out below, and both they and the Military Tasks are described in detail in Annex A.

THE MISSIONS OF THE ARMED FORCES

A: PEACETIME SECURITY

B: SECURITY OF THE OVERSEAS TERRITORIES

C: DEFENCE DIPLOMACY

D: SUPPORT TO WIDER BRITISH INTERESTS

E: PEACE SUPPORT AND HUMANITARIAN OPERATIONS

F: REGIONAL CONFLICT OUTSIDE THE NATO AREA

G: REGIONAL CONFLICT INSIDE THE NATO AREA

H: STRATEGIC ATTACK ON NATO

The most important changes from previous analyses are the establishment of Defence Diplomacy as a distinct Mission and the decision that we should no longer maintain forces solely to meet a strategic attack on NATO – an attack on the scale of the Cold War is no longer within the capacity of any conceivable opponent and to recreate such a capacity would take many years.

5.   The next step was to consider the level of forces or <u>scales of effort</u> over and above those required for day-to-day commitments (such as Northern Ireland) that we should plan to be able to contribute to different Missions, taking account of Britain's national interests, operational requirements, Allies' capabilities and our military strengths. These assumptions were also influenced by recent experience of operations, such as the Gulf Conflict, Bosnia and many smaller deployments, and an assessment of future trends and requirements. It should be emphasised that the scales of effort are planning tools; they do not prejudge the size of an actual commitment in particular contingencies, which could be larger or smaller depending on the circumstance. The principal scales are:

–   <u>small scale</u>: a deployment of battalion size or equivalent. Examples include the ARMILLA patrol in the Gulf, the British contribution to United Nations Forces in Cyprus (UNFICYP), and the Royal Air Force operations enforcing the no-fly zones over northern and southern Iraq;

–   <u>medium scale</u>: deployments of brigade size or equivalent for warfighting or other operations. An example would be our contribution to the NATO-led Intervention Force (IFOR) in Bosnia;

    – <u>large scale</u>: deployments of division size or equivalent. The nearest recent example would be our contribution to the Gulf War coalition, although on that occasion the British division deployed with only two of its three brigades. Large scale is the maximum size of force we would plan to be able to contribute to peace enforcement operations, or to regional conflicts outside the NATO area;

    – <u>very large scale and full scale</u>: these comprise all the forces we plan to make available to NATO to meet significant aggression against an Ally. This is the most serious single scenario that we might now face. The two scales differ primarily in the warning time available in response to the emergence of a major threat, and in the size of that threat. In both cases, we assess that the warning time we would have available would be many months or even years.

6.   We then considered the levels of <u>readiness</u> applicable to different sorts of operation: that is, the notice period within which units must be ready to deploy from their bases or other designated areas. The readiness required of a unit helps to determine its level of manning, equipment, training and logistic sustainability, and also whether it must be Regular or could be Reserve. The aim was to match readiness to political and military requirements, including warning times where applicable. Account has also been taken of campaign sequencing, or the phases in which operations are likely to unfold, recognising that the readiness of forces should be graduated in accordance with the likely timescales for their employment.

7.   Another important factor is the likely duration of operations and the potential need to sustain a deployment for an indefinite period – <u>endurance</u>. The possibility that some operations will be enduring (as in Cyprus, where we have taken part in UNFICYP since 1964, and more recently in Bosnia) has a significant impact on total force structure, as there must be sufficient units to be able to provide for the rotation of those actually deployed at any one time.

8.   We also considered the number of operations, of a given scale of effort and duration, that we should be able to conduct at any time – <u>concurrency</u>. This is crucial to determining the size and shape of force structure needed in the modern world, where military planning is no longer dominated by a single worst-case scenario. Our conclusion was that not to be able to conduct two medium scale operations at the same time would be an unacceptable constraint on our ability to discharge Britain's commitments and responsibilities. It would, for example, oblige us to withdraw from an enduring commitment such as Bosnia in order to respond to a second crisis.

9.   Finally, emerging trends in the relative importance of different aspects of defence capability were identified, to guide <u>force development</u> and ensure that our forces have the capabilities they will need, rather than those we needed in the past.

10.   Taking all these planning assumptions together, we concluded that the size and shape of our forces are dictated by two main requirements:

    – the challenge of conducting two concurrent medium scale operations – one a relatively short warfighting deployment, the other an enduring non-warfighting operation. For many elements of our force structure this is the most demanding scenario;

    – a full scale operation, which is the most demanding scenario for the remainder of the force structure.

11.   On the basis of the planning assumptions, we carried out an exhaustive analysis of the force elements required for each Military Task, and thus of the numbers of each force element required overall. The methodology used, the attribution of force elements to Military Tasks and the consequent numbers of each force element are set out in more detail at Annex A. The remainder of this essay sets out the main results of this process in terms of future force structure.

II   Future Force Structures and Capabilities

12.   <u>The nature of future operations – force projection</u>. For four decades following the Second World War, British military planning was dominated by the Cold War, in which it was expected that most ground and air forces would fight from or close to their peacetime bases, with the benefit of well-established infrastructure. This scenario envisaged a highly intense conflict of relatively short duration. By contrast, modern operations are likely, even in the worst case, to be smaller in scale; indeed, as explained above, the risk of a strategic attack on NATO is now so remote that we no longer need to maintain forces specifically for that contingency. But modern operations will often be <u>more</u> demanding in other ways. British Forces can expect to have to <u>go to</u> the operation, rather than have it come to them. They may have to operate in areas where the supporting infrastructure is limited or non-existent. And they may have to sustain non-warfighting operations for indefinite periods whilst retaining the ability to respond to other contingencies. This calls for rather different force projection capabilities than we have needed in the past.

13.   <u>Multinationality</u>. With the exception of national commitments such as Northern Ireland and the security of our Overseas Territories, future operations will almost always be multinational. Britain will usually be working as part of a NATO, UN or Western European Union (WEU) force, or an ad hoc "coalition of the willing". This means that we do not need to hold sufficient <u>national</u> capabilities for every eventuality, just as we did not plan to defeat the Warsaw Pact on our own. But it also means that we need balanced, coherent forces which are capable of operating effectively alongside forces from other countries (including in NATO's Rapid Reaction Corps, which Britain leads), and that this requirement must be reflected in training and equipment. Our conclusion is that an ability to make a contribution of this kind to multinational operations will enable us to meet our national commitments as well.

14.   <u>High-Intensity and Low-Intensity operations</u>. In the past, a contrast has sometimes been drawn between the high-intensity capabilities required for warfighting and the low-intensity capabilities which suffice for other operations such as peacekeeping – between, for instance, tanks on the one hand and light infantry in blue berets on the other. This is an artificial distinction. Recent experience has shown that enforcing and keeping the peace may require the deployment of forces trained for modern conventional warfare and equipped with battle-winning capabilities such as aircraft carriers, submarines, tanks, artillery, attack helicopter and combat aircraft. And the capabilities an operation requires may vary over time, as has been the case in Bosnia. We therefore need a balanced and coherent spectrum of capabilities, which collectively provide a range of deployment options.

15.   <u>Trends in military capabilities</u>. Our analysis of force development identified a number of increasingly important capabilities:

- command, control, communications and computers, and intelligence, surveillance, target acquisition and reconnaissance (ISTAR) are crucial to the exploitation of information to facilitate the effective employment of combat power;

- the trend towards force projection operations, for which we may need to deploy very rapidly in order to be successful, places an increasing premium on transport or lift capabilities;

- combat service support (logistics, equipment and medical support) is key to sustaining deployed operations, particularly those of significant duration;

- protection against chemical and biological weapons will be critically important in some of the regions in which we are likely to have to operate, such as the Gulf;

- Special Forces are likely to be essential in all warfighting operations;

- air manoeuvre forces will be increasingly central to high intensity land operations as their tempo continues to increase.

Some other capabilities remain very important, but improvements in the range and precision of weapons mean that we no longer need them in the same quantity as during the Cold War. And some capabilities are of declining relative importance. This applies in particular to the direct defence of the United Kingdom itself and to open-ocean maritime operations. In a number of cases, changes of emphasis are already in train. Elsewhere, the Review has re-balanced the force structure, to provide a coherent set of capabilities for the operations we now need to plan for.

Joint Rapid Reaction Forces

16.   Joint operations are one of the main themes of the Review. The most important development in the force structure is the creation of a pool of Joint Rapid Reaction Forces to bring together all readily available forces from the three Services. From this pool we will be able to draw the right force packages to mount short-notice brigade level or equivalent force projection operations of all kinds across the crisis spectrum. Joint Rapid Reaction Forces are described in full in the essay on joint operations, but the measures set out below should be seen in the context of the Joint Rapid Reaction Force concept.

Shortfalls

17.   The Review has given high priority to addressing shortfalls in our capability to undertake force projection operations.

18.   Strategic Lift. We cannot at present deploy Joint Rapid Reaction Forces quickly enough to meet operational requirements in the changed strategic environment, nor is commercial shipping or airlift likely to be available in sufficient quantities to meet rapid deployment deadlines, although it will have an important place in transporting follow-on forces. Our tactical capabilites are already being improved by introducing additional support helicopters and replacing our oldest Hercules aircraft by the new C-130J version. A wide range of options was considered for enhancing the strategic sea and air transport fleets. The following is the most effective alternative in military and resource terms:

  – acquire four additional roll-on roll-off container ships to join the two now entering service. It may be possible to do so using Public Private Partnership;

  – in the short term, meet our strategic airlift needs with four C-17 large aircraft or their equivalent;

  – in the longer term, we need to consider a suitable replacement for our remaining elderly transport aircraft, for which the proposed European Future Large Aircraft is a contender.

Bids will be invited to meet the short-term and long-term air transport requirements in parallel competitions. Requests for proposals will be issued later this year, and we would hope to make decisions on procurement by early 2000. We will also be issuing requests for information for a new tanker aircraft for air-to-air refuelling.

19.   Enhanced logistic support. The current logistic support structure cannot sustain prolonged or simultaneous operations. A package of measures will address the worst of these deficiencies by:

  – establishing two well-found logistic lines of communication to support two concurrent medium scale deployments;

  – creating a joint force logistics component commander and headquarters for each to co-ordinate joint support assets;

  – enhancing the ability of the Royal Air Force to conduct operations from remote locations with little or no infrastructure by providing the logistic support needed for deployed operating bases;

  – addressing key shortfalls in weapon systems and spares for critical equipments, including missiles and ammunition;

    – organising logistic support forces so that early-entry capabilities are provided by Regular personnel, with greater use of Reserve and contractor personnel for follow-on support once the operation has been established.

The overall effect of these measures will be to provide more effective support for deployed forces and to reduce the current overstretch problem faced by personnel in many logistic specialisations.

20.   <u>Enhanced medical support</u>. Medical support is another area in which there are serious shortfalls, both in peacetime care and in operational medical support. The Government will therefore make a significant investment in additional equipment and personnel. Key improvements will include:

    – establishment of a new Regular ambulance regiment;

    – the updating of current afloat medical support facilities;

    – acquisition of an additional 200-bed primary casualty receiving ship; and

    – enhanced ground and aeromedical evacuation capabilities.

To meet the requirement for extra medical personnel, the Regular element of the Defence Medical Services will be increased. But it is neither militarily sensible nor cost effective to rely solely on Regular personnel. We will therefore use the compulsory call-out of medical Reserves to augment Regular field hospitals for combat operations at the equivalent of brigade level or above. Work is under way to establish the best ways of achieving this.

Joint enabling capabilities

21.   The Review has sought to reflect and reinforce the increasingly joint nature of operations and the force structure. A number of capabilities common to more than one Service have a crucial enabling role:

    – significant improvements in tactical communications and command and control systems, such as the Joint Tactical Information Distribution System, the Joint Operational Command System, and the Theatre Wide Area Communications Network, are already in hand. To exploit this, we are creating a fully-equipped Joint Task Force Headquarters, capable of very rapid deployment for the command and control of our Joint Rapid Reaction Forces, and forming the nucleus of a second Headquarters which could take command of a separate, concurrent deployment;

    – continued investment in key ISTAR projects, such as the Astor airborne stand-off radar, the Phoenix remotely piloted vehicle and the Cobra counter-battery radar, will significantly improve the effectiveness of British forces in future conflicts;

    – we have confirmed plans to enhance the support helicopter force by procuring 22 Merlin support helicopters and 14 Chinook HC2A/3. Their overall military effectiveness will be increased by establishing a new Joint Helicopter Command to co-ordinate the use of all battlefield helicopters;

    – the Review has confirmed the importance of our highly-regarded Special Forces capability in a broad variety of roles, and we will continue to invest in high-quality personnel, training and equipment.

Maritime capabilities

22.   Maritime forces are inherently well suited to most force projection operations. Their reach, ability to sustain themselves without reliance on host nation support and flexibility are invaluable attributes. A joint maritime force often provides the opportunity for early and timely intervention in potential crises. Recent events in the Gulf have demonstrated the ability of maritime forces in this respect. In almost all operations, maritime forces will be essential

to help deliver ground forces to the theatre. And they can make a vital contribution to humanitarian and disaster relief operations, as seen recently in Montserrat.

23.   Against this background, the Review suggested a continuing shift in focus away from large-scale open-ocean warfare towards a wide range of operations in littoral areas. This reflects changes in the potential maritime threat, especially relative to NATO, the missions of our forces and the likely geographic location of future operations. These changes are a continuation of trends since the end of the Cold War. They include a decline in the likelihood of an open-ocean anti-submarine or anti-surface threat on the scale previously envisaged. Similarly, the size of the mine countermeasures force must take account of the reduced threat in home waters. By contrast, we need to be better able to conduct combat operations in littoral areas, to take better advantage of the contribution of maritime platforms in the force projection role, and to have the capacity to undertake prolonged peace support commitments and day-to-day tasks without overstretching our forces.

24.   To achieve this the Government will maintain strong and well- balanced maritime forces but with some changes of emphasis. The Strategic Defence Review will:

  - maintain plans to modernise the destroyer and frigate force with a new class of Common New Generation Frigates but reduce overall strength from 35 to 32 (this figure is based on two concurrent medium scale deployments, which is the most demanding requirement for the destroyer and frigate force);

  - continue modernisation of the nuclear-powered attack submarine force but reduce strength from 12 to ten in the longer term. All ten attack submarines will, however, be equipped to fire Tomahawk land attack missiles to increase their utility in force projection operations (this compares with previous plans to fit only seven submarines for the Tomahawk system);

  - modernise the mine countermeasures force and continue to increase its strength (currently 19 vessels), but limit the increase to 22 rather than 25 by paying off three older vessels;

  - maintain a full Commando Brigade and its specialist shipping, and continue the modernisation programme, which began with introduction of the helicopter carrier, HMS OCEAN, by procuring two landing platform docks and two landing ships logistic to replace current vessels;

  - retain all three Invincible Class aircraft carriers and their associated aircraft, and increase their utility by developing further their use by Royal Air Force as well as Royal Navy aircraft; and

  - continue plans to purchase 44 Merlin anti-submarine helicopters but place no further orders. In addition, ten Lynx Mk3 helicopters will be converted to Mk8 standard for operation from destroyers/frigates;

  - retain the comprehensive afloat support capability provided by the Royal Fleet Auxiliary, and continue planned modernisation by procuring two auxiliary oilers as replacements for the current vessels.

In addition, the dedicated fishery protection force will be reduced by one vessel following the decision of the Scottish Fisheries Protection Agency to move to the sole use of civil contractors to carry out this role in Scottish waters.

25.   This rebalancing will be matched by adjustments to peacetime tasks where necessary to ensure that overstretch is addressed. At the same time, we will take action to remedy longstanding undermanning within the Royal Navy. In the first instance, most personnel released by the changes set out above will be redeployed across the Service to ameliorate current shortfalls. Once manpower problems have been solved the net effect of the Review on the Navy's Regular manpower requirement will be a reduction of some 1,400.

26.   Future Aircraft Carriers and Carrier-borne aircraft. One of the key longer-term issues in the Review has been whether to replace the current generation of aircraft carriers and their aircraft, and if so with what. Our conclusion is that the ability to deploy offensive air power will be central to future force projection operations. But we cannot be certain that we will always have access to suitable air bases. Even when we do, experience has shown that bases may not always be available in the early stages of a crisis, and that their infrastructure is not always able to support the full

range of operations required. In these and a range of other operational circumstances, aircraft carriers can provide valuable flexibility. They can also offer a coercive presence which may forestall the need for warfighting, as recently in the Gulf. We judge that there is therefore a continuing need for Britain to have the capability offered by aircraft carriers.

27.   The Invincible Class carriers were designed for Cold War anti-submarine warfare operations with helicopters and a limited air defence capability provided by a small number of embarked Sea Harriers. This is no longer the main requirement. The emphasis is now on increased offensive air power, and an ability to operate the largest possible range of aircraft in the widest possible range of roles.

28.   When the current carrier force reaches the end of its planned life, we plan to replace it with two larger vessels. Work will now begin to refine our requirements but present thinking suggests that they might be of the order of 30,000-40,000 tonnes and capable of deploying up to 50 aircraft, including helicopters. Our intention is that they will be built using all relevant cost-saving techniques, following the example of HMS OCEAN. No decisions have been taken on a future carrier-borne aircraft but a version of the Joint Strike Fighter currently under development in the United States remains a strong contender. We are therefore participating in the concept demonstration phase of the programme.

29.   To get the maximum military output from this major investment, Royal Navy Sea Harrier FA2 and Royal Air Force Harrier GR7 aircraft will combine in a new force able to operate from land or carriers. Joint Force 2000 will be a significant upgrading of Britain's maritime force projection capability.

Land capabilities

30.   Both the Gulf Conflict and Bosnia have demonstrated that, notwithstanding technological advances, Britain still needs forces which can operate effectively on the ground, whether to enforce and keep the peace or to take and hold territory. Most of the warfighting capabilities used in the Gulf have also been required in Bosnia. The tempo of land operations is also increasing, putting a premium on forces which are deployable and mobile, but with sufficient protection and firepower for warfighting. The Army will therefore retain a balanced, combined arms, high capability structure of two deployable divisions, with some rebalancing to make existing forces more usable and to address overstretch in the current structure.

31.   At present there are five deployable brigades (three armoured and two mechanised) with wide utility, together with three lighter and more specialised deployable brigades (one airborne, one airmobile and the Royal Marines Commando Brigade). Our forces must be trained effectively for warfighting operations, available both as part of the Joint Rapid Reaction Forces and as part of NATO's ACE Rapid Reaction Corps, and able to undertake prolonged operations. This requires a balanced force structure and operational cycle, which we do not currently have. A force of six armoured and mechanised brigades achieves this and would improve significantly the Army's ability to deliver combat-ready formations. Because of its wider utility, a third mechanised brigade would also help to reduce overstretch, and we are therefore adopting this structure.

32.   In addition, we can no longer identify circumstances in which Britain would need to undertake parachute operations at greater than battalion group level. Maintaining a smaller battalion-level capability, which confers important operational flexibility, and modernising the role of the remainder of the Parachute Regiment to take advantage of their unique skills and ethos, has been central to the Review. We also need to make better use of key front-line equipment such as tanks.

33.   The Review will therefore make the following changes to the Army's operational structure:
   - 5 Airborne Brigade will be converted into a third mechanised brigade. The battalion-level airborne role will be transferred to 24 Airmobile Brigade which, when the Attack Helicopter enters service, will be developed into a new high capability air manoeuvre formation, forming part of the Joint Helicopter Command, and including two battalions of the Parachute Regiment;

- we will retain the ability to generate a division of three armoured brigades for warfighting operations, but adopt a militarily more effective structure for their component units. Instead of the eight small armoured regiments, each with 38 tanks and 470 personnel, planned previously, there will be six larger ones each with 58 tanks and 600 personnel. In parallel, the Army will adopt a "whole fleet management" approach to the tank fleet. Each regiment will hold only the 30 tanks it needs on a day-to-day basis to achieve required training standards. The balance required to bring regiments up to warfighting strength will be provided prior to deployment for operations. This will allow us to make better use of the new Challenger 2 tank fleet and reduce costs with no operational penalty;

- the two armoured regiments released as a result will be re-roled, one as the Army's contribution to the new joint capability for nuclear, biological and chemical defence, the other as a new armoured reconnaissance regiment;

- the current total of 40 Regular infantry battalions will be maintained but we will reconfigure them to reflect the creation of the third mechanised brigade. In future we will have:

  * nine instead of eight armoured infantry battalions,

  * six instead of four mechanised infantry battalions,

  * three parachute battalions of which one (rather than two as now) will be in-role at any time (the other battalions of the Parachute Regiment will be employed on other tasks), and

  * 22 instead of 25 light infantry battalions.

  Vehicles for the increased numbers of armoured and mechanised units will be made available by the more effective management of existing fleets;

- 15 Regular artillery regiments will be retained, although a light gun regiment will be re-roled to form a sixth AS90 regiment, and we will proceed with programmes for long-range precision munitions and for the Lightweight Mobile Artillery Weapon System;

- a sixth close support engineer regiment will be created, the engineer support provided to the air manoeuvre brigade will be increased from squadron to regiment level, and support to deployed air forces will be improved by forming two new Regular engineer squadrons and two new Regular signals squadrons;

- plans for future land weapon systems such as Medium Range TRIGAT and the Next Light Anti-Armour Weapon will be retained but planned numbers will be reduced to reflect the restructuring and changes to readiness.

34.   Basing in Germany. The Government is committed to the principle of NATO Allies stationing forces on one another's territory, which is an important symbol of our mutual obligations. Moreover, although the specific military argument for stationing forces close to the Cold War front line has disappeared, there are still significant military benefits in having capable forces based in continental Europe, where they are closer to many potential theatres of operations and they can train more readily alongside our Allies. There is also the practical and economic question of how much additional military infrastructure and training the United Kingdom could readily accommodate. All these considerations have led us to conclude that the bulk of our current military presence in Germany should remain there.

35.   Some reductions can, however, be made in that presence as part of Army restructuring. Three armoured regiments (including the two to be re-roled) and a number of supporting units will be removed from the front line in Germany and returned to the United Kingdom, totalling about 2,500 military personnel and some 186 tanks.

36.   Army Manpower. In overall terms, the size of the Regular Army will rise by some 3,300 personnel, with increases particularly in signals, engineer and logistics troops. Combined with the restructuring described above, we believe that this will eventually remedy overstretch in the force structure.

Air capabilities

37.   Air power remains a fundamental component of warfighting capability, complementing maritime and ground forces, and providing an offensive capability in its own right which will be enhanced by the increasing precision of air-delivered weapons. It has also proved its utility in non-warfighting operations, including the enforcement of no-fly zones and humanitarian deployments. The Review has concluded that Britain should therefore retain a balanced mix of aircraft, including offensive support, air defence, ISTAR and maritime patrol, airborne early warning, transport and tanker aircraft, and support and search and rescue helicopters. Our work has, however, identified a number of areas in which adjustments are necessary to reflect changes in the scale and readiness required for likely future operations.

38.   Most of the Royal Air Force front line will remain unchanged. The main decisions taken in the Review are as follows:

- most importantly, to maintain the Government's commitment to acquire 232 Eurofighters to replace the Tornado F3 and Jaguar in the air defence and offensive air support roles, with a front line establishment of around 140 aircraft. Eurofighter will be the primary component of the Royal Air Force future fighting capability and a vital element in Britain's overall defence effort;

- to retain in service all three types of offensive air support aircraft (Tornado GR, Harrier and – until replaced by Eurofighter – Jaguar) but reduce their front-line establishment from 177 to 154 aircraft, and from 14 to 13 squadrons. This reduction would comprise 12 Tornado GR1s, nine Harriers and two Jaguars. For operations carrying longer warning times we will continue to be able to increase the number of aircraft available by making use of the operational conversion units;

- to make a small reduction in the establishment of the Tornado F3 air defence force from 100 to 87 aircraft, and from six to five squadrons. We would again plan to make use of the operational conversion unit in some contingencies;

- continue with procurement of the Brimstone and Stormshadow air-to-surface missiles, and with plans to procure a beyond visual range air-to-air missile for the Eurofighter fleet;

- develop a new collision warning system for the Tornado GR4, to enter service early in the next century;

- make a small reduction in the RAF Regiment's squadron strength, from 14 to 13, but give them an enhanced nuclear, biological and chemical defence role as part of a new joint Service capability;

- maintain the search and rescue force and make it more cost-effective by greater use of civilianisation in non-deployable posts.

39.   As with the Royal Navy and the Army, the first priority for manpower released by these changes will be to reduce undermanning in the Royal Air Force as a whole. Once full manning has been achieved, the net effect of the Review on Regular RAF manpower will be broadly neutral.

40.   Future Offensive Air System. Future offensive air power requirements have been studied in conjunction with future aircraft carriers and carrier-borne aircraft. The proposals developed in the maritime context will meet a substantial part of Britain's overall future offensive airpower needs. There will, however, be an important requirement to replace in around 20 years' time the capability currently provided by the Tornado GR fleet in the offensive support role. No immediate decision is necessary on how we should do so, but we will continue to study how best to meet the requirement, giving consideration to cruise missiles and remotely piloted/unmanned air vehicles as well as manned aircraft.

Reserve Forces

41.　As noted above the risk of a strategic attack on NATO is now so remote that Britain does not need to maintain forces specifically against such a contingency. There is therefore no longer a requirement for large numbers of Reserves in this role. But recent experience, in the Gulf and in Bosnia, has underlined the value of the contribution the Reserves can make in operations from peace support to regional conflict. The Reserves also have a vital role in defence as a link between the Armed Forces and Society. The Reserves, and in particular the Territorial Army, will therefore continue to have a central part to play in Britain's defence. But to play that part effectively, they must change. If they do not, the Reserves face marginalisation and decline.

42.　The Government is determined that this will not happen and that the Reserves will not fade into our history. The Review will therefore:

- increase the strength of the Royal Naval Reserve (by about 350) and the Royal Air Force Reserve (by about 270), and make them even more usable;

- give the Territorial Army new roles, and integrate them more closely with the Regular Army. The primary emphasis will be on key support and medical tasks, making maximum use of the skills and enthusiasm that Reserve soldiers contribute;

- reduce the size of the Territorial Army from around 56,000 to a more compact and usable force of about 40,000;

- make more use of Territorial Army personnel across the spectrum of defence Missions, including through greater use of call-up to undertake force projection operations;

- establish a dedicated Army Mobilisation Centre to overcome problems experienced by Reservists in recent operations;

These changes are explained in greater detail in the separate essay on Reserve Forces.

Modern Forces for the Modern World

43.　The Government promised at the outset of the Strategic Defence Review that the process would be foreign policy-led, identifying what our forces need to be able to do and making sure that they had the necessary capabilities. This promise has been kept. We have identified the Missions and Military Tasks our forces must be able to undertake in support of Britain's foreign and security policy, and force structures have been derived directly from an analysis of those Tasks, informed by the planning assumptions we have developed and our strategic priorities. The Review has produced a clear and coherent force structure for Britain's Armed Forces in the next century.

Annex A to Future Military Capabilities Essay

Missions and Military Tasks

A1.   To ensure that the aims and objectives of foreign and security policy are properly reflected in defence planning, they need to be developed into specific functions for which the Armed Forces must be trained and equipped. Until recently, the Ministry of Defence planned to undertake three Defence Roles:

Defence Role One: to ensure the protection and security of the United Kingdom and our Dependent Territories even when there is no major external threat.

Defence Role Two: to insure against a major external threat to the United Kingdom and our Allies.

Defence Role Three: to contribute to promoting the United Kingdom's wider security interests through the maintenance of international peace and stability

These Roles were further broken down into some 50, more specific, Military Tasks.

A2.   Whilst the Defence Roles were a valuable step forward, their utility for detailed defence planning has lessened with the changes to the strategic environment in recent years. For example, they did not give sufficient prominence to the range of different operations covered by Role Three. We had already begun to move to an alternative approach based on Missions, and the Review has further developed and refined this. The eight Missions shown below provide a more accurate and balanced statement of what our Armed Forces are for, and a clearer and more coherent basis for defence planning. The Missions are deliberately not placed in any order of priority, and the sequence in which they appear has no significance for planning purposes.

THE MISSIONS OF THE ARMED FORCES

Defence policy requires the provision of forces with a high degree of military effectiveness, at sufficient readiness and with a clear sense of purpose, for conflict prevention, crisis management and combat operations. Their demonstrable capability, conventional and nuclear, is intended to act as an effective deterrent to a potential aggressor, both in peacetime and crisis. They must be able to undertake a range of Military Tasks to fulfil the Missions set out below, matched to changing strategic circumstances.

A: Peacetime Security: To provide forces needed in peacetime to ensure the protection and security of the United Kingdom, to assist as required with the evacuation of British nationals overseas, and to afford Military Aid to the Civil Authorities in the United Kingdom, including Military Aid to the Civil Power, Military Aid to Other Government Departments and Military Aid to the Civil Community.

B: Security of the Overseas Territories: To provide forces to meet any challenges to the external security of a British Overseas Territory (including overseas possessions and the Sovereign Base Areas) or to assist the civil authorities in meeting a challenge to internal security. (An amendment to legislation in due course will formalise the change of title from "Dependent Territories" to "Overseas Territories".)

C: Defence Diplomacy: To provide forces to meet the varied activities undertaken by the Ministry of Defence to dispel hostility, build and maintain trust, and assist in the development of democratically accountable armed forces (thereby making a significant contribution to conflict prevention and resolution).

D: Support to Wider British Interests: To provide forces to conduct activities to promote British interests, influence and standing abroad.

E: Peace Support and Humanitarian Operations: To contribute forces to operations other than war in support of British interests and international order and humanitarian principles, the latter most likely under UN auspices.

F: Regional Conflict Outside the NATO Area: To contribute forces for a regional conflict (but not an attack on NATO or one of its members) which, if unchecked, could adversely affect European security, or which could pose a serious threat to British interests elsewhere, or to international security. Operations are usually under UN or Organisation for Security Co-operation in Europe auspices.

G: Regional Conflict Inside the NATO Area: To provide forces needed to respond to a regional crisis or conflict involving a NATO ally who calls for assistance under Article 5 of the Washington Treaty.

H: Strategic Attack on NATO: To provide, within the expected warning and readiness preparation times, the forces required to counter a strategic attack against NATO.

A3.   For planning purposes, a further level of detail is needed below the Missions against which forces can be assigned. The concept of Military Tasks remains the best way of meeting this requirement. We have, however, sought to improve on previous attempts to define the functions of the Armed Forces by focusing as far as possible on outputs (such as peace enforcement) rather than inputs (such as the elements assigned to particular NATO force categories). In the process, we have also rationalised the set of Tasks, from 50 to 28. This does not imply that the Armed Forces have less to do! It simply reflects a more focused analysis, minimising the duplication which was a feature of the Tasks under the three Defence Roles.

A4.   The Military Tasks are set out below, with a short explanation of each. Although the Tasks are numbered for reference purposes, they are again not in any order of priority.

PEACETIME SECURITY

A5.   **MT1: Military Aid to the Civil Power in Great Britain**

Military Aid to the Civil Power in Great Britain is provided for the direct maintenance or restoration of law and order in situations beyond the capacity of the civil power to resolve in any other way.

A6.   **MT2: Military Aid to the Civil Power in Northern Ireland**

Military Aid to the Civil Power in Northern Ireland supports the Royal Ulster Constabulary in maintaining law and order and combating terrorism through the conduct of operations to deter terrorist activity.

A7.   **MT3: Counter Drugs Operations**

Military forces are made available upon request, where operational commitments and resources allow, to support the counter-drugs activities of law enforcement agencies in the United Kingdom and the Overseas Territories, and in support of the international counter-drugs effort.

A8.   **MT4: Military Aid to Other Government Departments**

Military Aid to Other Government Departments is the use of military forces for non-military Government tasks, including fishery protection and hydrographic tasks.

A9.   **MT5: Military Aid to the Civil Community**

Military Aid to the Civil Community is the provision of Service personnel and equipment, both in emergencies and in routine situations, to assist the community at large.

A10.   MT6: Military Search and Rescue in Peacetime

The Armed Forces provide a 24-hour peacetime search and rescue capability, with the priority task of rescuing Service personnel in the United Kingdom and surrounding seas. Search and Rescue for the civil community is provided in conjunction with other relevant agencies.

A11.   MT7: Nuclear Accident Response

The Department maintains a capability for nuclear accident response to ensure, in conjunction with civil agencies, an effective response to incidents or accidents in the United Kingdom involving nuclear weapons, defence nuclear materials or naval reactors; and, when requested, to provide assistance to civil authorities in accidents with civil nuclear facilities.

A12.   MT8: Integrity of United Kingdom Waters in Peacetime

To demonstrate British sovereignty within and ensure the integrity of the United Kingdom's territorial waters (and where necessary to protect the United Kingdom's rights and interests in the surrounding seas), a military presence is maintained which provides routine sea and air surveillance of these waters in peacetime.

A13.   MT9: Integrity of United Kingdom Airspace in Peacetime

A continuous recognised air picture and an air policing capability is needed to maintain the integrity of the United Kingdom's airspace, and meet NATO commitments in the United Kingdom Air Defence Region.

A14.   MT10: Intelligence

Defence intelligence collection, processing and analytical capability is required to support policy makers, planners and operational commanders.

A15.   MT11: Hydrographic, Geographic and Meteorological Services

Hydrographic surveying and geographic mapping and survey services are a defence responsibility because of the security aspects of providing hydrographic support for the strategic deterrent, anti-submarine warfare and mine countermeasures operations, and the need to maintain a survey capability for operations and emergencies. The Meteorological Office provides essential meteorological services and weather forecasts for the Armed Forces; and undertakes meteorological and climate research activities in order to retain Britain's world class reputation in meteorology.

A16.   MT12: Evacuation of British Citizens Overseas

In cases where civil contingency plans prove insufficient, defence capabilities held for other purposes may be used to evacuate United Kingdom entitled personnel from countries where their lives may be at risk.

A17.   MT13: Public Duties and VIP Transport

The Department provides military personnel for state ceremonial and routine public duties, and secure air transport for the use of the Royal Family and senior members of the Government.

SECURITY OF THE OVERSEAS TERRITORIES

A18.   MT14: Security of the Overseas Territories

The Ministry of Defence is responsible for the external security of Britain's Overseas Territories, and provides support and assistance to the civil authorities as required.

A19.   **MT15: Security of the Cyprus Sovereign Base Areas and Territorial Waters**

The British presence in the Sovereign Base Areas of Cyprus provides strategic communications facilities, a base for operations in the Eastern Mediterranean and beyond, military search and rescue, and training facilities.

DEFENCE DIPLOMACY

A20.   **MT16: Arms Control, Non-Proliferation, and Confidence and Security Building Measures**

The Ministry of Defence provides military and civilian personnel in support of arms control, non-proliferation and confidence and security-building regimes. It also supports export control regimes and arrangements. In addition, the Ministry of Defence is responsible for ensuring that Britain retains the ability to achieve political and military objectives despite the presence, threat or use of nuclear, biological or chemical weapons and their means of delivery.

A21.   **MT17: Outreach**

The Outreach programme is designed to contribute to security and stability in Central and Eastern Europe, the Caucasus and Central Asia through bilateral assistance to and co-operation with the countries concerned.

A22.   **MT18: Other Defence Diplomacy Activities**

The Ministry of Defence undertakes military assistance activities with overseas military forces and defence communities (not already covered under the Outreach programme under MT17) to help to dispel hostility, build and maintain trust, and assist in the development of democratically accountable armed forces.

SUPPORT TO WIDER BRITISH INTERESTS

A23.   **MT19: Support to Wider British Interests**

The Ministry of Defence conducts activities to promote British interests, influence and standing abroad, including in relation to Brunei, the Five Power Defence Arrangements and support to defence exports.

PEACE SUPPORT AND HUMANITARIAN OPERATIONS

A24.   **MT20: Humanitarian Operations and Disaster Relief Outside the United Kingdom and Overseas Territories**

Humanitarian crises and disasters, if not addressed rapidly and effectively at an early stage, can often lead to potentially serious conflicts. When appropriate, and at the request of the Foreign and Commonwealth Office or Department for International Development, the Armed Forces contribute to humanitarian and disaster relief operations, either on a national basis or as part of a co-ordinated international effort.

A25.   **MT21: Peacekeeping; MT22: Peace Enforcement**

Prevention, containment and resolution of conflict is a vital element in the maintenance of international stability and security. We will therefore make an appropriate contribution, in concert with other nations, to both peacekeeping and peace enforcement operations. Peacekeeping operations are conducted with the consent of the disputing parties in order to support the achievement of a long term peace settlement. Peace enforcement operations are conducted in circumstances where there is no peace or peace process to which all the relevant parties are committed; such operations are coercive in nature, and require warfighting capabilities sufficient to ensure compliance.

REGIONAL CONFLICT OUTSIDE THE NATO AREA

A26.   MT23: Regional Conflict outside the NATO Area

Inter-state conflicts may arise, outside the territory of NATO members, to which Britain may wish to respond along with other countries, to support other allies and partners, to protect our national interests, and to uphold international law and stability.

REGIONAL CONFLICT INSIDE THE NATO AREA

A27.   MT24: Regional Conflict inside the NATO Area; MT25: Major Regional Conflict inside the NATO Area

Under Article 5 of the Washington Treaty, Britain would assist any NATO Ally or Allies under armed attack in Europe or North America by taking appropriate action, including the use of armed force. Britain's force planning to meet this commitment is based on the contingency of a regional conflict involving aggression against a NATO member. This may include the predeployment and reinforcement of forces during a time of tension in order to deter aggression. The distinction between the two Tasks reflects the different scales of threat which potential future adversaries could pose in a regional context. The full range of Britain's military capabilities, including our nuclear forces, is available to NATO.

A28.   MT26: Military Home Defence

The Government has an obligation to ensure the provision of critical services and the functioning of government itself during times of crisis and conflict. This is achieved primarily by the protection of critical installations and information systems.

A29.   MT27: Nuclear Forces

Britain's Trident force provides an operationally independent strategic and sub-strategic nuclear capability in support of NATO's strategy of war prevention and as the ultimate guarantee of our national security. In current circumstances, nuclear forces continue to make a unique contribution to ensuring stability and preventing crisis escalation. They also help guard against any possible re-emergence of a strategic scale threat to our security.

STRATEGIC ATTACK ON NATO

A30.   MT28: Strategic Attack on NATO

This Task is concerned with the very remote risk of the emergence of a massive military threat to NATO territory, with the ability to mount major offensive operations on two or more fronts. In the current security environment, no forces are maintained specifically against it, although we retain the ability to reconstitute forces in the event of the emergence of such a major threat.

Determining the force structure

A31.   To determine the conventional forces required to carry out these Missions, we used a process of assigning force elements to Military Tasks known as force summation. This process identified forces committed to a Task at any one time (such as infantry battalions deployed in Northern Ireland) and those held contingent for a Task (such as infantry battalions which might need to be deployed as part of our commitment to NATO). It produced the total requirement for each force element, taking account of judgements about the requirements of each Military Task, and the main scale of effort and concurrency permutations discussed in the main essay. The total requirement for each force element was determined by the largest figure derived from these permutations. The main factors driving the force structure proved to be two concurrent medium scale operations or a single full scale operation. Readiness assumptions were then applied to establish which force elements must be Regular and which could be Reserves.

A32.   Finally, a range of additional factors were used to take account of our experience of the numbers actually required to produce the force structure needed for operations. These factors comprise:

- generation – for the Royal Navy this covers ships engaged in the training and trials needed to prepare for operations, for the Army it reflects differences between peacetime and wartime establishments (e.g. an armoured infantry battalion comprises three rifle companies in peacetime but would deploy for warfighting with four companies), and for the Royal Air Force, the fact that aircraft are used more intensively when deployed on operations means that more crews and additional aircraft are required to complete the training task in peacetime, so in order to deploy a given number of aircraft on operations, a higher number is required in peacetime (the crew/airframe ratio is 1.33:1 in peacetime, 1.5:1 for non-warfighting deployments and 2.0:1 for combat operations);

- maintenance – this reflects the Royal Navy's refit cycle and the average number of ships in refit at any one time;

- rotation – to maintain a commitment for a prolonged period while ensuring operational effectiveness and without placing undue strain on the personnel concerned, we must maintain a pool of forces to rotate through the deployed force. Experience shows that the optimum ratio for prolonged commitments is in the region of three or four ships, five army units and three or four RAF squadrons for each one deployed. We have assumed that these guidelines would be breached in the event of major warfighting operations or for two concurrent medium scale operations;

- regeneration – this applies to combat aircraft and reflects our ability to use operational conversion units, in an operational role, primarily in the event of a major NATO regional conflict for which there would be a prolonged period of warning time, but also for some sustained commitments;

- choice – for some Military Tasks we need to maintain a range of capabilities to reflect possible alternative requirements (e.g. a package of combat aircraft might need to focus on air defence, offensive air support or a mixture of the two).

A33.   As a supplement to force summation, we also used a scenario-based analysis to assess the forces necessary for force projection operations at medium and large scales of effort. This process was known as force estimation. It employed a range of contingencies, some based on recent operations, and the results were used to validate the force summation process.

A34.   The force structure resulting from the force summation work is set out in the three sets of tables in Annex B, together with the factors from which they have been derived:

- the first set assigns force elements to Military Tasks, and indicates whether they are committed or contingent to that Task. The table does not show those Military Tasks which have no forces specifically assigned to them. Nor does it cover MT10: Intelligence, which has been excluded for security reasons;

- the second set shows the number of each force element required to undertake the two main scale of effort and concurrency permutations – two medium scale deployments and a full scale deployment. They also show the impact of continuing other commitments in parallel and the factors discussed in paragraph A32 above. Royal Navy and combat aircraft totals have been rounded to the nearest whole number;

- the third set summarises for each force element the numbers held now and those that will be held once the Review has been implemented.

Annex B to Future Military Capabilities Essay

FORCE ELEMENT TABLES

GENERAL NOTES

The tables show planned post-SDR implementation force levels.

Only Regular Army Force Elements are shown as the revised structure of the Territorial Army has yet to be determined.

The Infantry Battalions Force Element covers all infantry tasks, some of which are planned to be undertaken by other units out of role, e.g. Armoured and Artillery Regiments and RM Commandos. The Force Element also includes the Armour Delivery role which will be undertaken by forces drawn from Infantry Battalions.

Engineer Regiments include the Military Works Force.

Equipment Support Battalions (REME) exclude the REME Battalion (Aviation) but include the REME Battalion in Northern Ireland.

The Royal Logistics Corps Regiments (Close and General Support) Force Element includes the Logistics Battalions supporting 24 Airmobile Brigade and 3 Cdo Brigade and the resident Regiment in Northern Ireland.

The Support Helicopters Force Element covers Puma, Chinook, Sea King 4 and Merlin Mk3 Support Helicopters. As these helicopter types vary in terms of range, endurance and carrying capacity we have expressed all numbers in terms of Chinook equivalents.

Mission: Peacetime Security
MTs 1 to 7

Force Element	Military Aid to the Civil Authorities MTs 1, 3, 4 & 5		Military Aid to the Civil Power in NI MT 2		Search and Rescue MT6		Nuclear Accident Response M17	
	Cttd	Cont	Cttd	Cont	Cttd	Cont	Cttd	Cont
Aircraft Carriers								
Amphibious Ships								
Attack Submarines		1						
Destroyers and Frigates		3				1		1
Minewarfare Vessels	4	1	3					
RM Commando								
Royal Fleet Auxiliary Vessels		1						
Strategic Deterrent Submarines								
Armrd & Recce Regiments								
Army Air Corps Regiments			1					
Artillery Regiments								
Engineer Regiments		1	1.33					
Equipment Support Battalions (REME)			1					
Field Hospital								
Infantry Battalions		1	12[1]	1				
NBC Regiment								
Royal Logistics Corps Regiments (Close and General Support)			1					
Airborne Early Warning Aircraft		1				1		
Air Defence Aircraft		2				2		
Maritime and Reconnaissance Aircraft		3		2		6		1
Offensive Air Support Aircraft		1						1
RAF Regiment Squadrons (Field and Rapier)			1					1
Support Helicopters		6.91	4.5	2				1.25
Transport and Tanker Aircraft		7		5		1		6

(1)   Total of infantry tasks, not all of which would be carried out by Infantry Battalions.

Mission: Peacetime Security
MTs 8 & 9, 12 & 13

Force Element	Integrity of UK Waters and Airspace MTs 8 & 9		Evacuation of British Citizens MT 12		Public Duties and VIP Support MT 13	
	Cttd	Cont	Cttd	Cont	Cttd	Cont
Aircraft Carriers				1		
Amphibious Ships				7		
Attack Submarines				2		
Destroyers and Frigates		3(1)		4		
Minewarfare Vessels		4		4		
RM Commando				3		
Royal Fleet Auxiliary Vessels				6		
Strategic Deterrent Submarines						
Armrd & Recce Regiments				0.33	(2)	
Army Air Corps Regiments						
Artillery Regiments				2	(2)	
Engineer Regiments				1.33		
Equipment Support Battalions (REME)						
Field Hospital				0.5		
Infantry Battalions				2	3.25	
NBC Regiment						
Royal Logistics Corps Regiments (Close and General Support)				2		
Airborne Early Warning Aircraft		2		2		
Air Defence Aircraft	2			18		
Maritime and Reconnaissance Aircraft		12		5		2
Offensive Air Support Aircraft				18		
RAF Regiment Squadrons (Field and Rapier)				4	1	
Support Helicopters				19		
Transport and Tanker Aircraft		1		51		

(1)   Part of the deployed force at Full Scale.

(2)   The Household Cavalry Mounted Regiment and King's Troop Royal Horse Artillery are committed to Public Duties but are not included here because they do not contribute to any other MTs and are not included in the force levels.

MT 10: Intelligence - not shown for security reasons.

MT 11: Hydrographic - not shown because the units principally involved are not shown in the list of Force Elements.

Mission: Security of the Overseas Territories
MTs 14 & 15

Force Element	Security of Overseas Territories including Cyprus MTs 14&15	
	Committed	Contingent
Aircraft Carriers		1
Amphibious Ships		8
Attack Submarines		3
Destroyers and Frigates	2	9
Minewarfare Vessels		6
RM Commando		3
Royal Fleet Auxiliary Vessels	2	8
Strategic Deterrent Submarines		
Armrd & Recce Regiments		1.33
Army Air Corps Regiments		1
Artillery Regiments		2
Engineer Regiments	0.49	4.66
Equipment Support Battalions (REME)		
Field Hospital		2
Infantry Battalions	2	3
NBC Regiment		
Royal Logistics Corps Regiments (Close and General Support)		3
Airborne Early Warning Aircraft		3
Air Defence Aircraft	4	33
Maritime and Reconnaissance Aircraft		5
Offensive Air Support Aircraft		42
RAF Regiment Squadrons (Field and Rapier)	1	5
Support Helicopters	1	26.50
Transport and Tanker Aircraft	2	62

Mission: Support to Wider British Interests
MT 19

Force Element	Support to Wider British Interests MT 19	
	Committed	Contingent
Aircraft Carriers		
Amphibious Ships		5
Attack Submarines		1
Destroyers and Frigates		2
Minewarfare Vessels		
RM Commando		1
Royal Fleet Auxiliary Vessels		3
Strategic Deterrent Submarines		
Armrd & Recce Regiments		0.66
Army Air Corps Regiments		
Artillery Regiments		1
Engineer Regiments		1
Equipment Support Battalions (REME)		
Field Hospital		
Infantry Battalions	1	2
NBC Regiment		
Royal Logistics Corps Regiments (Close and General Support)		1
Airborne Early Warning Aircraft		1
Air Defence Aircraft		6
Maritime and Reconnaissance Aircraft		2
Offensive Air Support Aircraft		
RAF Regiment Squadrons (Field and Rapier)		1
Support Helicopters		0.75
Transport and Tanker Aircraft		45

Mission: Peace Support & Humanitarian Operations
MTs 21 & 22

Force Element	Peace Keeping MT 21		Peace Enforcement MT 22	
	Committed	Contingent	Committed	Contingent
Aircraft Carriers		1		2
Amphibious Ships		6		9[1]
Attack Submarines		1		3
Destroyers and Frigates		4	2	13
Minewarfare Vessels		4		8
RM Commando		1		3
Royal Fleet Auxiliary Vessels		5	1	8
Strategic Deterrent Submarines				
Armrd & Recce Regiments		1.66		9
Army Air Corps Regiments		0.33		4
Artillery Regiments		1		13
Engineer Regiments		1.44		9.66
Equipment Support Battalions (REME)		1.2		6
Field Hospital		0.5		3
Infantry Battalions	1	2		15
NBC Regiment				1
Royal Logistics Corps Regiments (Close and General Support)		1		3.5
Airborne Early Warning Aircraft		2		5
Air Defence Aircraft		14		33
Maritime and Reconnaissance Aircraft		5		10
Offensive Air Support Aircraft		24		74
RAF Regiment Squadrons (Field and Rapier)		1		9
Support Helicopters		20.5		47
Transport and Tanker Aircraft		51		82

(1)   Second helicopter carrier could be provided by Aircraft Carrier in helicopter carrier role.

Mission: Regional Conflict Outside the NATO Area
MT 23

Force Element	Regional conflict Outside NATO MT 23	
	Committed	Contingent
Aircraft Carriers		2
Amphibious Ships		9[1]
Attack Submarines		3
Destroyers and Frigates		13
Minewarfare Vessels		8
RM Commando		3
Royal Fleet Auxiliary Vessels		8
Strategic Deterrent Submarines		
Armrd & Recce Regiments		9
Army Air Corps Regiments		4
Artillery Regiments		13
Engineer Regiments		9.66
Equipment Support Battalions (REME)		6
Field Hospital		3
Infantry Battalions		15
NBC Regiment		1
Royal Logistics Corps Regiments (Close and General Support)		3.5
Airborne Early Warning Aircraft		5
Air Defence Aircraft		33
Maritime and Reconnaissance Aircraft		10
Offensive Air Support Aircraft		74
RAF Regiment Squadrons (Field and Rapier)		9
Support Helicopters		47
Transport and Tanker Aircraft		82

(1)   Second helicopter carrier could be provided by Aircraft Carrier in helicopter carrier role.

Mission: Regional Conflict Inside the NATO Area
MTs 24 & 25, 26, 27

Force Element	Regional Conflict Inside NATO and Military Home defence MTs 24, 25 & 26		Nuclear Forces MT 27	
	Committed	Contingent	Committed	Contingent
Aircraft Carriers		2		
Amphibious Ships		9[1]		
Attack Submarines		4[2]	2	1
Destroyers and Frigates	2[3]	23[4]	1	2
Minewarfare Vessels	2	15	1	3
RM Commando		3	0.5	
Royal Fleet Auxiliary Vessels		12	1	
Strategic Deterrent Submarines			1	3
Armrd & Recce Regiments		10		
Army Air Corps Regiments		4		
Artillery Regiments		13		
Engineer Regiments		9.66		
Equipment Support Battalions (REME)		6		
Field Hospital		3		
Infantry Battalions		24		5[5]
NBC Regiment		1		
Royal Logistics Corps Regiments (Close and General Support)		6		
Airborne Early Warning Aircraft		6		
Air Defence Aircraft		42		2[6]
Maritime and Reconnaissance Aircraft		11	4	8
Offensive Air Support Aircraft		92		
RAF Regiment Squadrons (Field and Rapier)		10		
Support Helicopters		52.25		
Transport and Tanker Aircraft		82		

(1)   Second helicopter carrier could be provided by Aircraft Carrier in helicopter carrier role.
(2)   Includes one for strategic intelligence.
(3)   Committed vessels are NATO Standing Forces. These vessels would be included within the deployed force at Full Scale.
(4)   Deployed force at Full Scale.
(5)   Counted as part of deployed force.
(6)   Same aircraft as for MT 8 Integrity of UK Airspace.

CONCURRENCY: TWO CONCURRENT MEDIUM SCALE

Force Element	ENDURING NON-WARFIGHTING	ONE-SHOT WARFIGHTING	CONTINUING COMMITMENTS	FACTORS	TOTAL
Aircraft Carriers	1	1			2 [1]
Amphibious Ships	6 [2]	8 [2]			8 [2]
Attack Submarines	1	4 [3]	2	3.36	10
Destroyers and Frigates	4	9	1	18.13	32
Minewarfare Vessels	4	6	5	3.24	18
RM Commando	1 [2]	3 [2]	0.5	1	3.5 [2]
Royal Fleet Auxiliary Vessels	5	8	1	1.26	15
Strategic Deterrent Submarines			4		4
Armrd & Recce Regiments	1.66	2.66		4	8.33
Army Air Corps Regiments	0.33	3	1	0.33	4.66
Artillery Regiments	1	2.33		4	7.33
Engineer Regiments	1.44	3.33	1.66	5.10	11.53
Equipment Support Battatlion (REME)	1.2	2	1	2.8	7
Field Hospital	0.5	1		1	2.5
Infantry Battalions	3	3	15 [4]	34 [4]	55 [4]
NBC Regiment		0.55			0.55
Royal Logistics Corps Regiments (Close and General Support)	1	1	1	3	6
Airborne Early Warning Aircraft	2	3			5
Air Defence Aircraft	14	17	6	33	70 [5]
Maritime and Reconnaissance Aircraft	5	5	4	8	22
Offensive Air Support Aircraft	24	42		88	154
RAF Regiment Squadrons (Field and Rapier)	1	7	3	2	13
Support Helicopters	20.5	26.5	7.5	9.75	64.25
Transport and Tanker Aircraft	51 [6]	82 [6]			82

(1) Currently a third Aircraft Carrier is required to maintain two available for operations.
(2) Only one amphibious operation at any one time is planned, therefore no Medium Scale concurrency is assumed.
(3) Includes one for strategic intelligence.
(4) This reflects the number of infantry tasks in Northern Ireland. However, as explained above, units from other arms are available to fill some of these tasks, thus reducing the requirement for infantry battalions to 40.
(5) Would require the use of operational conversion unit aircraft.
(6) It is assumed that the deployment timings of two concurrent Medium Scale deployments will be staggered meaning that concurrency requirements for transport aircraft at Medium Scale will not arise.

CONCURRENCY: FULL SCALE

Force Element	FULL SCALE	CONTINUING COMMITMENTS	FACTORS	TOTAL
Aircraft Carriers	2			2 [1]
Amphibious Ships	9 [2]			9 [2]
Attack Submarines	4 [3]	3	3.36	10
Destroyers and Frigates	26	3	0.27	29
Minewarfare Vessels	17	4	1.08	22
RM Commando	3	0.5		3.5
Royal Fleet Auxiliary Vessels	12	1	0.09	13
Strategic Deterrent Submarines		4		4
Armrd & Recce Regiments	10			10
Army Air Corps Regiments	4	1		5
Artillery Regiments	13		2	15
Engineer Regiments	9.66	1.33	2	13
Equipment Support Battalions (REME)	6	1		7
Field Hospital	3			3
Infantry Battalions	29	8	3	40
NBC Regiment	1			1
Royal Logistics Corps Regiments (Close and General Support)	6	1		7
Airborne Early Warning Aircraft	6			6
Air Defence Aircraft	42	2	43	87 [4]
Maritime and Reconnaissance Aircraft	11	12		23
Offensive Air Support Aircraft	92		92	184 [4]
RAF Regiment Squadrons (Field and Rapier)	10	1		11
Support Helicopters	52.25	4.5		56.75
Transport and Tanker Aircraft	82			82

(1)   Currently a third Aircraft Carrier is required to maintain two available for operations.
(2)   Second helicopter carrier could be provided by Aircraft Carrier in helicopter carrier role.
(3)   Includes one for strategic intelligence.
(4)   Would require the use of operational conversion unit aircraft.

Force Levels

Force Element	Previously Planned Force Level	Planned Force Level Post-SDR	Difference
Aircraft Carriers	3	3[1]	[1]
Amphibious Ships	8	8	
Attack Submarines	12	10[2]	-2
Destroyers and Frigates	35	32	-3
Minewarfare Vessels	25[3]	22[3]	-3
RM Commando	3.5	3.5	
Royal Fleet Auxiliary Vessels	15	15	
Strategic Deterrent Submarines	4	4	
Armrd & Recce Regiments	11	10	-1
Army Air Corps Regiments	5	5	
Artillery Regiments	15	15	
Engineer Regiments	11	13	+2
Equipment Support Battalions (REME)	6	7	+1
Field Hospital	3	3	
Infantry Battalions	40	40	
NBC Regiment	[4]	1	+1
Royal Logistics Corps Regiments (Close and General Support)	8	7	-1
Airborne Early Warning Aircraft	6	6	
Air Defence Aircraft	100	87	-13
Maritime and Reconnaissance Aircraft	23[5]	23[5]	
Offensive Air Support Aircraft	177	154	-23
RAF Regiment Squadrons (Field and Rapier)	14	13	-1
Support Helicopters	63[6]	63[6]	
Transport and Tanker Aircraft	78	82	+4

(1) We plan to replace the INVINCIBLE Class with two larger vessels in the longer term.
(2) Staged reduction from initial force of 12.
(3) Force level is currently 19.
(4) NBC Regiment was planned to be provided by the Territorial Army.
(5) Force level when Nimrod MRA4 replaces Nimrod MR2.
(6) Chinook-equivalents: actual number of Support Helicopters planned is 116.

SUPPORTING ESSAY SEVEN
RESERVE FORCES

1.   Britain relies heavily on the contribution made by Reserves to our Armed Forces. Reservists serve alongside their Regular colleagues in operations, and they are integral to our ability to expand our forces in times of crisis. They are a very cost-effective way of adding to our military capabilities. One of the clearest findings of the Defence Review has been that we could not fight a war at any significant level without them.

2.   There are several kinds of Reservist. The two largest groups are the Regular Reserves: former members of the regular Armed Forces who are still liable for service in an emergency; and the part time Volunteer Reserves, who are recruited directly from the civilian community – the Royal Naval Reserve, the Royal Marines Reserve, the Territorial Army and the Royal Auxiliary Air Force. However, the Reserve Forces Act 1996 also provides for the wider use of Reserves, such as those wishing to serve full time with the Regular Forces for a limited period, and "sponsored" Reserves: contractors' staff who have agreed to be mobilised when required, to continue their work in operations alongside the Service personnel who depend upon them. These newer forms of reserve service may well become more important in future.

3.   The Volunteer Reserves are more widely distributed across the country than the Regular Forces. In most areas, it is therefore Volunteer Reserves who provide the most visible Armed Forces presence. They help to inform society about what the Armed Forces do and of their importance to the nation, and provide a means by which the community as a whole can contribute to our national security interests. The role of cadet forces also establishes a vital link with young people, fostering good relations and helping recruitment.

4.   Our aim in the SDR has been to ensure that the roles given to Reserve Forces are relevant to the international situations in which our Armed Forces might operate in the future. We need to ensure that the Reserves are usable, and that in common with the rest of the Armed Forces they have the right training, the right equipment, and the right support to play their part. We also need to ensure that the administration and support of the Reserve Forces is efficient and effective, and that the link between Reserves and Regular Forces at all levels is strong and clear.

5.   We have concluded that it is right for Britain to continue to remain dependent on our Reserve forces. But these Reserve forces, which have hitherto largely been held for a struggle for national survival, should be restructured to undertake new challenges and the new style of operations that may be launched in the future.

The Cold War and its aftermath

6.   The size and shape of our Reserve Forces is governed by the risks that we face. During the Cold War, our forces were organised to defend against a strategic attack on Western Europe. We were required to maintain a large Reserve so as to regenerate our forces on the continent in the face of such aggression, and to defend the United Kingdom against direct attack. The size of our Armed Forces, both Regular and Reserve, grew over the last decade of the Cold War, and the Reserves expanded significantly faster than our Regular Forces.

7.   With the welcome end of the Cold War, there has been a period of adjustment in all three Services:

   a. the Royal Naval Reserve reduced in size by 1994 to less than half of its Cold War establishment, and changed role from focusing on mine countermeasures (with dedicated vessels) and defence of the UK base to a wider role in support of the Fleet. However, its utility has been limited by relatively low levels of funding for training activity. Royal Marines Reserve authorised strength fell from 1,580 to 1,000 in the same period;

b. the <u>Territorial Army</u> has been restructured twice, falling in strength from 74,000 in 1989 to around 56,000 in 1998. An increasing proportion of the Territorial Army is involved in vital supporting roles, rather than combat ones. But large numbers of Reservists in the Territorial Army are still dedicated to Military Home Defence, such as the guarding of key points throughout Britain or forming a reconnaissance screen against an invading force;

c. the <u>Royal Auxiliary Air Force</u> had also reduced in size by 1994 to less than two-thirds of its Cold War establishment.

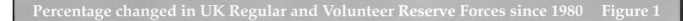

Percentage changed in UK Regular and Volunteer Reserve Forces since 1980   Figure 1

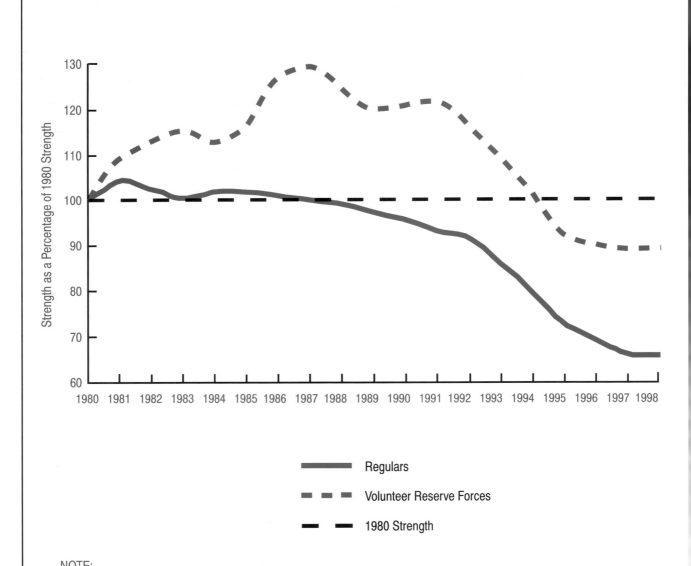

NOTE:
Volunteer Reserve Forces include Home Service Force and Non-Regular Permanent Staff.

Strategic Defence Review

The Requirement

8.   The key element of the changed strategic situation is that there is no longer any immediate threat of a major conventional attack on Britain or on our NATO allies; nor could such a threat re-emerge without warning and preparation time of some years. On the other hand, the likelihood of short notice, smaller-scale conflicts around the world has increased. Taken together, this means that the forces we have available to deploy can be smaller than before, but they will have to be more flexible and more ready to deploy at very short notice. They will also have to be able to sustain operations for extended periods.

The Future Reserve Role

9.   Against this background we have concluded that the main contribution of Reserves should switch from being insurance against a struggle for national survival to supporting Regular Forces' deployments abroad, both with individuals and with formed units.

10.   Certain individuals in the Reserves will need to be ready to reinforce Regular units with their special skills, wherever required. They will therefore need to be held at similar – sometimes very short notice – readiness to their Regular colleagues. Many of these individuals will be drawn from the Regular Reserves, but some will be from the Volunteer Reserves.

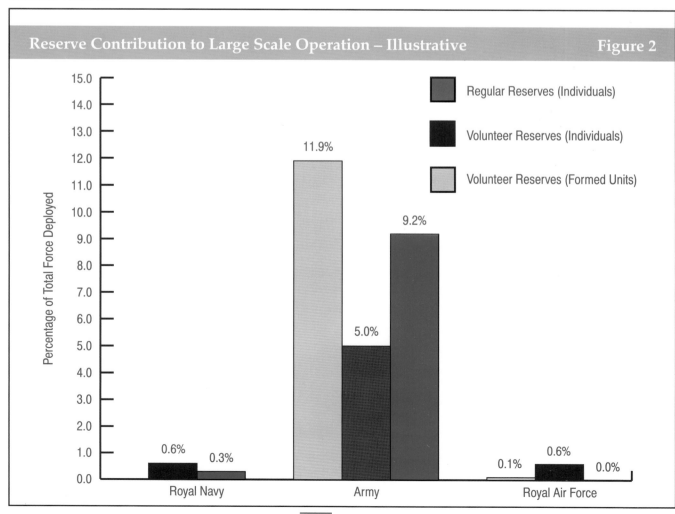

Reserve Contribution to Large Scale Operation – Illustrative   Figure 2

11.   In general, <u>Reserve Units</u> would require a period of warning and preparation before they could deploy. But we believe that they could also be ready, in time, to perform a wide range of specialist supporting tasks for large and very demanding operations (such as the Gulf War of 1990/1): these, too, may occur at relatively short notice. All this means that we will need Reserves that can be fully integrated into Regular formations and able to work with high levels of skill in situations that may be very demanding.

12.   We also consider that Reserves should be able to serve in long running peace support operations, of the kind now taking place in Cyprus or Bosnia, that have become part of the Armed Forces' day to day work. These types of operations have increased in number over the past decade and we have benefited greatly from the willingness of several thousand Volunteer and Regular Reservists to support current operations and valued their commitment and skills.

13.   There is another factor we need to bear in mind: the scope for Reservists, many of whom are in civilian employment, to provide continuous support to the Regular Forces is understandably limited; this means that, unsurprisingly, the overwhelming majority of the burden of these commitments must continue to fall on the Regular Forces.

14.   In all of the roles described above, the requirement for Reserves is likely to remain broadly steady or to increase. But given the disappearance of a direct threat, there will not be the same requirement for large numbers of the Territorial Army committed to Military Home Defence. There are also a few cases where roles currently performed by Volunteer Reserve units are likely to be required at such short notice that we must now plan for their tasks to be fulfilled by regulars.

The Size of Volunteer Reserve Forces

15.   To respond to these new circumstances we are proposing the following changes:

The Royal Naval Reserve

16.   The Royal Naval Reserve ceiling will increase by 10% from 3,500 to 3,850 to provide an expanded pool of personnel available for use across the Fleet. These trained personnel will be available for augmenting the Royal Navy. No changes are planned to the strengths or roles of the Royal Marines Reserve.

The Territorial Army

17.   There needs to be substantial change to the composition and structure of the Territorial Army, especially to reflect the clear requirement to provide highly trained and properly resourced forces to support the Regular Army while reducing the effort devoted to the old Military Home Defence task. The following are the key changes proposed:

   a. we shall need more medical Reserves, as part of our overall aim of increasing medical support to the Armed Forces generally;

   b. we shall continue to require Reserves in a wide range of arms to support the Regular Army on operations;

   c. we shall need fewer light infantry battalions and Royal Armoured Corps (also known as "Yeomanry") regiments. We also plan to reduce the number of engineer and transport regiments, some of which currently exist to support a rather larger force than we are now likely to deploy.

These changes will produce a Territorial Army of about 40,000 volunteers. This is smaller than the present structure, but differs in that it is specifically constructed to meet our current and foreseeable future requirements. Most importantly, the Territorial Army will have a meaningful and clearly defined function – and one which the nation will need to rely on if our Armed Forces are to perform their tasks as effectively in the future as they have in the past. Work on the detailed design, structure and composition of the Territorial Army will be carried forward during the autumn.

The Reserve Air Forces

18.   Following the reductions in 1994, the Reserve Air Forces had already begun to be reconfigured and this was under way before the Strategic Defence Review was undertaken. Among other things, the RAF is committed to the employment of Reservist aircrew in support of the front line, and a significant number have already taken part in Air Transport operations. The Review has also identified the need for an additional 270 posts within the Reserve Air Forces in other supporting roles.

Readiness

19.   Numbers of Reserves and the roles they undertake are important. But the key to the future effectiveness of the Reserve Forces is readiness – being properly prepared so that units and individuals in the Reserves will be able to do the job required of them in the right timescale. Currently most of our Volunteer Reserves are at low levels of readiness; in the future some units, particularly logistic, medical and other support elements, will be placed at higher states of readiness to reflect the increased likelihood that they will be called out. Already, all Reserve aircrew and Public Relations personnel – and a significant proportion of Intelligence personnel – in the Reserve Air Forces are now High Readiness Reserves, liable to deploy on operations within days.

Call-out Arrangements

20.   Reserves in the future will be there to be used, with clearly defined and important roles. If they are to be used properly we must be able to deliver the Reserves to where we need them in the right timescale. This means that there must be better arrangements for call-out. In other words, such is the importance of Reserves that we must be able to have great assurance as to their availability. We believe that improvements to our existing procedures are necessary in these new circumstances. In the Territorial Army, for those who volunteer for service in operations, we will invest much more effort in mobilisation, so as to ensure that there is a smooth process that will deliver individual Reservists to units, capable of making an immediate contribution. To this end we are establishing an Army Mobilisation Centre and new management measures to improve the quality of service and training to Reservists on call-out, on operations, and on return to civilian life.

21.   In some circumstances, however, it will not be possible to rely upon Reservists volunteering. In mounting any major operation we will need to guarantee the availability of key capabilities provided by the Reserves, whether these are in battalions, sub-units, or the skills of a particular individual, and we will need to do so within a short period of time. Although many individual Reservists may be willing to volunteer for service, for a range of reasons some will not, and it is unlikely to be enough to rely on this willingness alone; nor would it be fair on Reservists or on their comrades.

22.   If we are to use our Reserve Forces to their maximum effect on any sizeable operation, we must therefore be prepared to mobilise them compulsorily. Selective compulsory call-out is therefore envisaged for situations well short of a direct threat to the United Kingdom – for example, for deployments on a similar scale to the Gulf War.

The Reserves Commitment

23.   Planning for our Reserves to take part in force projection operations underlines our seriousness about the use of Reserves, and their importance. In turn it demands from those in the Reserves a commitment to the possibility of active service. Membership of the Reserve Forces implies taking a share in the responsibility for the fulfilment of our defence and foreign policy objectives. All Reservists must be available and expect to be mobilised under the 1996 Reserve Forces Act. We will be emphasising to our volunteers the seriousness of their responsibilities in this regard.

Employers

24.   For our part, we recognise that this will make demands on those who employ Reservists as well as on the volunteers themselves. The appeal and financial payment provisions of the Reserve Forces Act 1996 will help us to address such concerns. We will seek, in a continuing dialogue with civilian employers, to reinforce support for the Reserves and to encourage it at all levels in the community. We will depend heavily upon the excellent work of National and other Employer Liaison Committees, and the Territorial, Auxiliary and Volunteer Reserve Associations (TAVRAs). We have been encouraged, in the course of the Review, by the many expressions of support received from employers for the Reserve Forces, and recognition they show of the benefits that staff with Reserve experience bring to any organisation.

Resources

25.   Since such clear and crucial roles for the Reserves have been identified in the Review, we recognise that it is vital that Reserves are resourced to carry them out. Sufficient funds must be made available to ensure that all Reserve units are properly manned and trained to meet the tasks required of them, and are capable of using new equipment with familiarity and confidence in an operational situation. We are determined to provide the resources necessary. In particular, new equipment will be introduced as part of our continuing programme of improving the capability of our Armed Forces; and training days will be provided at a level sufficient to guarantee operational effectiveness and to make service in the Reserves a challenging and enriching experience.

26.   We therefore intend that training for the Royal Naval Reserve and the Royal Marines Reserve will increase, in the case of the Royal Naval Reserve by 40% and for Royal Marines Reserve recruits by 66%. Territorial Army members volunteering for service with Regular Forces will have two weeks focused training immediately following mobilisation. And we intend that in the future the resourcing of our Reserves will continue to get the attention it deserves.

Local Links

27.   As well as providing the opportunity to contribute to the effectiveness of the Armed Forces, service in the Reserves has wider social and representational benefits, in that it offers the opportunity to people from all walks of life and in all areas to make a contribution to the national good. Such links benefit both sides. Volunteers bring back technical and management skills to industry, improved citizenship to society, and assist in regional support in many ways, including recent military aid to flooded areas.

28.   The Reserves provide important support to the cadets. The cadet forces are significant national volunteer youth movements. We aim to plan the changes to the Reserve Forces in such a way as to minimise any disruption to

the cadets. In addition, we intend there to be modest increases in resources devoted to cadets from the defence budget.

29.   All this will make implementing the changes to the Reserves, and to the Territorial Army in particular, a very complex process. It may not be until some months after our initial announcements that we will be able to make clear how each Territorial Army unit and training centre may be affected. However, the principles we will apply in restructuring the Territorial Army will take local issues very much into account. We will want to protect, so far as possible, existing strong links with the community, and with the cadet forces. We will want to build upon the enthusiasm there is in many areas for volunteer service. We will also want to take into account matters such as the availability of training facilities, and the need for close working between Territorial Army units and the Regular Armed Forces. Within these constraints, we aim to preserve as wide a presence of the Territorial Army throughout the country as possible.

Administration and Career Management

30.   We have taken the opportunity to consider our arrangements for the day-to-day running of our Reserve Forces. It is important that Reserve Forces should be backed up by a policy-making and administrative structure which is efficient, which ensures that the linkage between Reserve Forces and the Regular Forces alongside whom they will serve in battle is properly managed, and which at the same time recognises the special circumstances relating to service in the Reserves.

31.   Support to Reserves is therefore to be enhanced by a dedicated manning and careers branch for the Territorial Army, which has now opened at the Army Personnel Centre in Glasgow. Similar functions are already conducted in the much smaller Reserves of the other Services. A clearly defined structure for high-level policy direction for the Territorial Army is now in place, and work on a range of initiatives is under way. This will ensure that issues relating to the Territorial Army are given sufficient prominence at the very heart of the Army's policy-making processes, that the new focus for the Territorial Army set out in the Review will be driven through successfully, and that the full resources of the Ministry of Defence are placed behind Reservists.

The TAVRAs

32.   At local level administration and support of the major elements of the Reserve Forces will continue to be carried out through the TAVRAs, working within the context described in the 1996 Reserve Forces Act. This is a tri-Service role which has been carried out by the TAVRAs and their predecessor organisations for many years. It is an unusual arrangement, but has been found to be a successful one. The TAVRA system ensures that people from the local communities in which the Reserve Forces and cadets are based are involved in the running of Reserve and cadet units. It also provides Reserve Forces and cadets representatives with the right of direct access to Ministers, so that they can make representation about Reserves issues. This provides an important balance and ensures that the case for the Reserves is clearly articulated at a high level.

33.   TAVRAs have a second role as administrators and suppliers of services to the Reserve and cadet forces organisations. All this will remain unchanged. However, to reflect the increasing operational integration of Army Reserve and Regular forces, there will be certain changes in the way in which TAVRAs are organised (they were last restructured in 1968). It is important that regional commanders take on full responsibility for the operational standards of Army Reserve units in their area; as a result, TAVRA boundaries will be altered and brought more in line with the Army's Regular command structure. The new arrangement will take account of the needs of the other Services' Reserve Forces and all the cadet organisations. There are areas of activity, such as property management and recruiting, where the Royal Naval Reserve and Royal Marines Reserve will rely more heavily on the assistance of the TAVRAs, where this is seen to be beneficial and cost-effective.

Conclusion

34.   We need the Reserves: they have a proud history and we fully intend that they will have a secure and relevant future. We need the commitment of tens of thousands of individuals to train for and take part in military operations in support of our legitimate national interests and foreign policy objectives. There is great flexibility in the Reserves, both in the type of service and in the wide range of roles a Reservist may fill. There are many ways that Reservists can and will make their contribution in future. Without them we will not be able to do much that our Armed Forces might be called on to do.

35.   The Strategic Defence Review has given us the opportunity to restructure our Reserve Forces in a coherent and enduring way. It has confirmed the need for them to continue to perform some existing roles and to take on new and demanding ones. But it has also shown where some Cold War tasks are no longer relevant. We consider that the size and shape of the Reserve Forces emerging from the Review will be sufficient to meet any plausible operational eventuality.

36.   There will, in particular, be changes to many Army regiments that have long and honourable histories. This, we recognise, will be hard for many involved. But the resulting forces will be capable and usable – better fitted and able to work in support of Regular Forces on all types of operations. With the commitment of individual Reservists and their employers, the right training, support and equipment and new management arrangements, our Reserve Forces will be more important, more relevant, and will provide their volunteers with opportunities to continue serving the country in ways that are both meaningful and necessary.

SUPPORTING ESSAY EIGHT
JOINT OPERATIONS

1.   In joint operations, the forces provided by two or more Services are integrated to maximise their combined military effectiveness. Using military capabilities jointly is fundamental to modern warfare. The extension and encouragement of our ability to conduct joint operations successfully has therefore been at the heart of the Strategic Defence Review, and the principles have been set out in a Joint Vision Statement.

JOINT VISION STATEMENT

- Success in modern warfare depends on joint teamwork. Battles and wars are won by maritime, ground and air forces operating effectively together in support of shared military objectives.

- Joint operations are not new and Britain's Armed Forces have a proud record of successful co-operation. In the modern world, where we will face complex and unexpected situations which require a swift and flexible response, the importance of a joint approach is more critical than ever.

- Individual units depend for their fighting capability on the training, discipline and ethos generated by their parent Service. But success for the force as a whole requires effective orchestration of its individual components.

- To achieve this, a single joint commander is needed, supported by a unified command structure. The joint commander must be able to draw upon and direct the entire range of front-line forces committed to the operation, together with supporting units and personnel (both military and civilian).

- Joint teamwork does not just happen. It requires a shared understanding of the roles each participant is required to play. It also needs mutual confidence, built up from extensive practical experience of operating together, that everyone will deliver his or her contribution effectively.

- We must therefore ensure that a joint approach forms a central part of the way defence activity is carried out. This means closer integration in day-to-day training, in operations, and in the way defence is organised, supported and managed at all levels.

- The future of Britain's defence is in joint operations. We must therefore create an integrated framework which, while capitalising on single-Service professionalism, will be increasingly and necessarily joint.

---

2.   The Joint Vision will help to shape the future organisation and operations of the Armed Forces. It will guide developments in strategy, doctrine, technology and force structure. This essay describes the basis from which the joint or integrated concept will be developed, and the specific measures forming part of the Review.

The Starting Point – A Joint Inheritance

3.   Because of our geography, joint operations have always been fundamental to British military success. Much of our planning for the Cold War was undertaken on a joint basis, and this stood us in good stead in the Falklands, the Gulf and Bosnia. But the requirement is changing all the time. What was adequate during the Cold War is inadequate in today's very different circumstances. The traditional distinction between ground, sea and air theatres of operations is rapidly being replaced by a single battlespace, embracing all three environments and cyberspace, and encompassing functions as diverse as joint logistics, information warfare and media operations. Britain's Armed Forces have an unparalleled tradition of joint co-operation, on which we now intend to build to produce truly integrated forces for the next century.

4.   The post-Cold War process of increasing joint co-operation and integration between the Services started during the mid-1990s:

- a Permanent Joint Headquarters has been established at Northwood. It now plans and executes all joint operations, including Bosnia and recent deployments to the Gulf;

–   a Joint Rapid Deployment Force was set up to provide a national quick response capability;

–   the Joint Services Command and Staff Course at Bracknell has started to train future commanders in a completely joint environment;

–   a start has been made in expanding integration in the support area, including joint flying training establishments at Barkston Heath and Shawbury; and joint fixed- and rotary-wing aircraft repair organisations run by the Royal Air Force and Royal Navy respectively; and

–   we have deployed forces on operations in fully joint packages, such as the mixed Navy and Royal Air Force air wings serving aboard the aircraft carrier sent to the Gulf earlier this year.

The Way Ahead – The Strategic Defence Review

5.   Although these initiatives are helping to foster a culture of joint operations, the changes have not yet gone far enough. The Strategic Defence Review will therefore carry the joint approach to defence forward where it makes sense to do so in the front-line, the command structure and the support area.

6.   There will, however, be no merger of the Services. Our judgement and experience elsewhere is that this would reduce, not increase, their overall effectiveness. Within a joint framework, the individual Services have distinct roles and professional skills. This has been reflected throughout the SDR work, which has been based firmly on practicalities rather than dogma, taking account of the lessons learnt on operations and the views of our own personnel.

Joint Rapid Reaction Forces

7.   Today's unpredictable strategic environment is placing new demands on the Armed Forces. If they are to play an effective role in supporting Britain's foreign and security policy objectives, their ability to conduct a wide range of military activities, over long distances and often at short notice, will be paramount. We concluded early in the Review that we needed broadly the same kind of forces to meet contingencies arising from our vital stake in European security, our very important interests in the surrounding regions, and our wider national and international responsibilities elsewhere. We also concluded that these forces must be flexible, high capability, mobile and responsive, with the training, motivation and equipment to be successful in demanding conventional warfare and complex peace support operations.

8.   Such forces must be able to send a powerful message of our willingness to act should diplomacy fail. As United Nations Secretary General Kofi Annan said recently: ". . . . you can do a lot more [with diplomacy] when it is backed up by firmness and force".

9.   The creation of hard-hitting, flexible and genuinely deployable forces, able to undertake the full spectrum of short- notice missions in today's international environment, became a central theme of the Review. And our analysis made it clear that to be effective, these forces must be joint.

10.   The Joint Rapid Deployment Force was an important step in the right direction. It brought together capabilities drawn from all three Services into a joint structure for short notice operations in which NATO was not involved. These capabilities included light ground forces (the Commando and airborne brigades), heavier ground forces at battalion level, and a range of maritime and air forces. Creating a pool of readily available forces from all three Services was clearly right. It has also provided a good focus for developing our joint operational expertise.

11.   But experience has revealed some major flaws in the concept:

- the Force, especially its ground component, lacked the self-protection, tactical mobility and firepower needed for more intense combat operations. And its reinforcement would have been a long time coming because of our limited strategic transport capabilities;

- the Force was a one-shot weapon. It had only a single logistic and medical support chain so that it could conduct only one operation at a time. In the post Cold War world, we cannot expect to be able to meet our commitments and responsibilities consecutively rather than concurrently. One of the consequences has been a reluctance to use the Joint Rapid Deployment Force in some crises because, once committed, our ability to respond quickly elsewhere would be constrained;

- the force did not have genuinely joint deployable headquarters; and

- the force as such did not have a NATO role, which risked creating unhelpful distinctions between different types of operation and giving the incorrect impression to our Allies that we were beginning to re-nationalise our defence policy.

12.   The Strategic Defence Review has acknowledged the strengths of the Joint Rapid Deployment Force and sought to build on them. Our aim has been more capable, better supported joint forces with the strategic transport to make them truly deployable.

13.   The solution we have adopted is a pool of Joint Rapid Reaction Forces, bringing together all readily available forces from all three Services, including a range of enhanced capabilities to address the deficiencies described earlier. From this pool we can draw the right force packages to mount short-notice medium-scale (i.e. brigade size or equivalent) operations of all kinds across the crisis spectrum and under NATO, Western European Union, UN coalition or national auspices. We will be able to mount concurrent operations if necessary, or use the pool of forces to make a coherent and balanced early contribution to larger operations, subsequently building up our commitment over time using forces held at lower readiness levels. The concept is set out diagrammatically in *FIGURE 1* below.

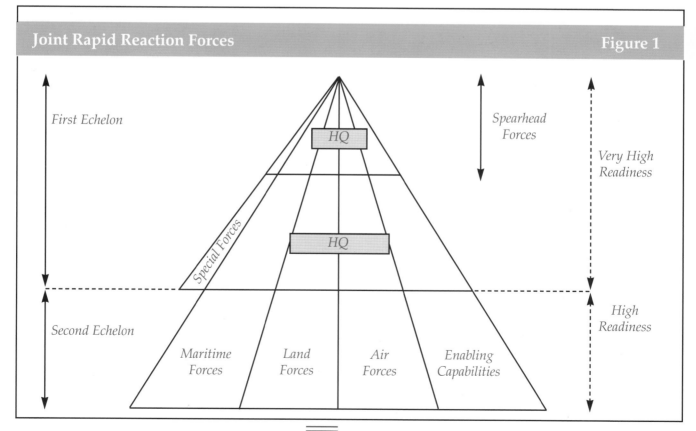

Joint Rapid Reaction Forces   **Figure 1**

14.   To be effective, the Joint Rapid Reaction Forces concept requires a significant increase in the size of our pool of readily available joint forces, including front line, command, support and transport capabilities. Among the key additions will be the airmobile brigade (and, in due course, its successor air manoeuvre brigade); an armoured and a mechanised brigade; much larger and more capable maritime and air elements; special forces; a dedicated joint task force headquarters, properly manned, equipped and trained, together with the nucleus of a second such headquarters for concurrent operations; logistic, medical and other support to mount two concurrent operations; heavy lift aircraft and four further roll-on/roll-off container ships. As a result, instead of being limited to deploying a light brigade, reinforced by a battalion of heavier troops, we will for example be able to send a commando brigade to take part in a peace support operation and an armoured brigade to contribute to a warfighting mission elsewhere. Or vice versa, depending on the circumstances.

15.   The Joint Rapid Reaction Forces will be ready to deploy in two echelons, supported by a range of enabling capabilities. The planned composition of these forces is set out in the following boxes.

ENABLING CAPABILITIES

Whatever the size of force package deployed, several key 'enabling capabilities' will be required. These include:

–   command and control (including a deployable joint task force headquarters), joint communications and information systems, intelligence support, and administrative support;

–   joint logistics support, including deployed medical support; and

–   strategic transport – usually provided by MOD-controlled transport assets for first echelon forces, and by a combination of MOD and commercially contracted strategic transport assets for follow-on forces.

THE FIRST ECHELON

First echelon forces will be available at very high readiness. The most readily available elements of the first echelon will be 'Spearhead Forces'. The pool will include:

–   Special Forces;

–   an attack submarine, surface warships and a support ship;

–   a spearhead battlegroup based on a light infantry battalion or commando group, drawn from 3 Commando Brigade, 3(UK) Mechanised Division's 'ready brigade' or 24 Airmobile Brigade; and

–   a mix of offensive and defensive combat aircraft, reconnaissance aircraft, helicopters, short-range air defence units and supporting tactical air transport and air-to-air refuelling aircraft.

The balance of first echelon forces could be drawn from:

–   additional Special Forces;

–   shipping to generate a maritime task group centred on an aircraft carrier or helicopter assault ship, and including amphibious shipping if necessary to support the lead Commando battlegroup;

–   lead battlegroups, to provide a broad choice of capabilities, including:
    *   a lead Commando battlegroup equipped with Lynx anti-tank helicopters (Longbow Apache when in service), support helicopters and all-terrain vehicles;

* a lead parachute battlegroup, based on a parachute battalion;
* a lead aviation/armoured reconnaissance battlegroup, with Lynx anti-tank helicopters (Longbow Apache when in service), armoured reconnaissance and infantry sub-units;
* a lead armoured battlegroup with Challenger tanks and Warrior armoured infantry vehicles; and
* combat support and logistic support groups with artillery, air defence, engineer and other assets;

– a range of high capability air assets, including additional offensive and defensive combat aircraft, helicopters and support aircraft.

THE SECOND ECHELON

The second echelon of forces will be available at high readiness to provide more substantial capabilities should the first echelon require strengthening or to conduct subsequent operations. These forces would probably use a combination of MOD and commercially contracted transport assets to deploy. The pool would comprise:

– additional maritime forces to form a second or larger, more capable maritime task group, including an amphibious capability if necessary to support 3 Commando Brigade;

– a choice of ground force brigades drawn from:
* 3 Commando Brigade, including specialist capabilities for amphibious, mountain and cold weather operations;
* a mechanised 'ready brigade' from 3 (UK) Mechanised Division;
* an armoured 'ready brigade' from 1 (UK) Armoured Division; and
* 24 Airmobile Brigade, providing an aviation, parachuting or tactical air-landed capability;

– substantial additional air assets to enable operations across the full spectrum of airpower roles to provide a robust air contribution to the Joint Task Force.

16.   The pool of forces available for the Joint Rapid Reaction Forces will vary from time-to-time but its approximate size and shape will include:

– around 20 major warships (aircraft carriers, attack submarines, amphibious ships, destroyers or frigates);
– about 22 other vessels (mine warfare and support ships);
– four ground force brigades;
– about 110 combat aircraft;
– over 160 other aircraft.

17.   Setting up the Joint Rapid Reaction Forces is a major undertaking, but we believe that this initiative is right for defence and that the logic underpinning it will command widespread agreement. Taken together, the measures we propose will provide Britain with a step-change in our ability to undertake short- notice force projection operations.

18.   It will take time to put all of the capabilities in place. We are, however, giving priority to this aspect of implementation of the Strategic Defence Review, and our aim is for the Joint Rapid Reaction Forces to be operational in 2001.

Chief of Joint Operations

19.   In parallel, we are pressing forward with the move to greater joint co-operation and integration in a number of other key areas. The substantial expansion in both the number and types of forces assigned to our Joint Rapid Reaction Forces, and hence the increasing number of operations likely to come under the command of the Permanent Joint Headquarters, has led us to reassess the role of the Chief of Joint Operations.

20.   As explained in our Joint Vision, his role is crucial to operational success. And units operate more effectively if they have exercised regularly as a joint force and if they are familiar with the commanders, headquarters and joint procedures under which they will work on operations. To ensure that the contingency plans and joint procedures are effective in a wide range of potential scenarios, there is a need regularly to bring together key Joint Rapid Reaction Force commanders and their personnel.

21.   We will therefore increase the responsibilities of the Chief of Joint Operations. He will have increased authority for enhancing the training and preparedness of the Joint Rapid Reaction Forces. A new two-star post, the Chief of Joint Force Operations and Training, will be established to assist him in these tasks. The Chief of Joint Operations will also have a much greater voice in stating joint warfare requirements. And he will be responsible for a top level budget, placing him on a similar budgetary footing to the single Service Commanders in Chief.

Joint Force 2000

22.   The operational potential of a joint carrier air wing was graphically shown earlier this year in the Gulf, when the deployment of Royal Air Force Harrier GR7s alongside the Royal Navy Sea Harriers on HMS INVINCIBLE made an important contribution to the multinational force applying pressure on Iraq to comply with UN resolutions.

23.   Total integration of current Harrier aircraft into a single force is impracticable. The two Harrier variants share only around 10% of their airframe and avionics, and they have quite different primary operational roles. But closer harmonization between the existing Harrier forces could pave the way towards a truly joint force for the future. Capitalising on the success of current joint Harrier operations, we propose to develop a Joint Force 2000, which could eventually involve the replacement of all Harriers with a common aircraft type.

24.   There are several options for the new aircraft (which would be capable of operating from ashore and afloat). For the Joint Force 2000 concept to work successfully, we will need a common aircraft, common operating procedures, common maintenance practice and a common support organisation. Further study will begin shortly to determine the best way to realise the potential which the concept offers to provide a flexible and deployable joint force, able to operate either from land bases or aircraft carriers.

Joint Defence Centre

25.   The importance of joint operations has highlighted the need for greater cohesion and better co-ordination in the development of joint doctrine. Such doctrine provides guidance for the planning and conduct of joint operations and training at all levels.

26.   We will therefore set up a Joint Defence Centre to develop high-level joint doctrine, co-ordinate the development of single Service doctrine, and provide the British input to Allied and multi-national doctrine. It will also support the operational role undertaken by the Permanent Joint Headquarters. The Centre will give impetus to forward

thinking, contribute to the future joint vision and strategic development of our armed forces and thus contribute directly to the cohesion and effectiveness of our forces in joint operations. Work is in hand to establish where the Centre should be situated.

Joint Helicopter Command

27.   Our work has emphasised the need for joint approaches to capability areas in which more than one Service is directly involved. One of the main examples is battlefield helicopters. All three Services operate battlefield helicopters in support of forces on the ground; these include the Royal Navy's Sea Kings; the Army's Lynx and Gazelles (and Longbow Apache when in service); and the Royal Air Force fleet of Chinooks, Pumas and Wessex (and Merlin Mk3 when in service). Other helicopters are employed in anti-submarine warfare/anti-surface warfare, airborne early warning and search and rescue roles. But their roles and the equipment they use have little in common with battlefield helicopters.

28.   Operational experience in Northern Ireland, Bosnia and the Gulf has demonstrated the unique contribution of battlefield helicopters throughout the conflict spectrum. Moreover, it has become evident that there are frequently too few of them available to meet the collective demands they face.

29.   One option which has frequently been discussed is the transfer of all battlefield helicopters to a single Service. But, as with merger of the Services, we believe that any advantages would be outweighed by the damaging impact it would have on ethos, morale and operational effectiveness.

30.   We therefore propose to form a Joint Helicopter Command, responsible for training, standards, doctrinal development and support for operations. The Command will draw on the equipment, personnel and expertise of the single Services and be charged with providing the Joint Force Commander tailored packages of battlefield helicopters (from one or more Service), support equipment and personnel, to meet operational requirements. The Command will provide a single focus for the ready transfer of best practice from Service to Service and for removing, over time, differences in current operating procedures.

31.   Significant rationalisation of the engineering and supply arrangements for helicopter operations has already taken place in recent years. The Defence Helicopter Support Authority has become the tri-Service organisation for the management of all helicopter support, and its responsibility will be expanded to include the direction and tasking of the non-deployable elements of helicopter support in each Service. This will help develop a taut customer/supplier relationship with the new Joint Helicopter Command.

32.   Further study is now underway to determine the best location for the new Command's Headquarters, and its detailed responsibilities. Our assessment is that this initiative will produce small savings and that, in time, the new Command will provide the framework for much greater efficiency and operational effectiveness.

Joint Ground Based Air Defence

33.   A second area where greater joint integration can produce important operational benefits is ground based air defence. Our deployed forces continue to require low level air defence cover to protect manoeuvring ground troops and key static installations such as logistic sites and air bases. Until now, both the Army and the Royal Air Force have maintained separate capabilities using different variants of the Rapier short-range air defence missile system. Each used their own operating procedures, command and control systems, maintenance support chains and training organizations. This has been operationally inflexible and wasteful.

34.   In the future, Rapier training will be conducted jointly at RAF Honington and the differing variants of the system will be phased out and replaced by a common standard by 2006. This will allow a Joint Air Defence Headquarters to contribute specialist staff to the joint commander of air defence operations, and to organize training and support. These measures will ensure that joint deployments will have a properly integrated and flexible low level air defence coverage, as well as achieving greater efficiency, particularly in Rapier training and support.

Joint Nuclear, Chemical and Biological Defence

35.   Joint integration can be especially effective in response to new or emerging threats. The continuing global proliferation of weapons of mass destruction and recent events in the Gulf have underlined the risks which deployed forces may face from these weapons, particularly biological and chemical, and the consequent need for an effective and deployable nuclear, biological and chemical defence capability.

36.   Training is already conducted jointly at the Nuclear, Biological and Chemical Defence Centre at Winterbourne Gunner, but we shall now build on this by establishing a joint (Army and Royal Air Force) nuclear, biological and chemical defence regiment manned mainly by Regular personnel. This contrasts with the current capability, which is provided by the Territorial Army. Through this joint approach the unit will be able to provide this essential capability at the high readiness necessary to support the deployments of our Joint Rapid Reaction Forces. The pooling of expertise, together with a new joint doctrine, will allow for this capability to be flexibly deployed to protect all forces as the threat dictates.

Joint Support

37.   Joint co-operation and integration can have benefits throughout defence, in the support area as well as the front line. The joint approach is increasingly at the heart of modern, effective and efficient support. It will also help us move towards a functional, defence-wide support structure, which makes increasing sense in the modern world and will help us to free resources for other defence priorities.

38.   One of the most obvious areas in which we need a joint approach is support to deployed forces. For example, in providing communications support, the Army and Royal Air Force have maintained their own units based in Britain (at RAF Digby) and Cyprus. These have been collocated but we have decided that in future they should become Joint Service Signal Units, to provide more effective support to joint operations of all kinds. This will also enable us to rationalise their organisational structure.

39.   The same principle applies fundamentally to logistic support. Our current logistic support organisations were developed to support forces from a single Service, operating predominantly from secure bases with the necessary infrastructure already in place. Recent experience in the Gulf, Bosnia and operations in Africa has shown that at present we have difficulty in supporting diverse, joint operations mounted from sparsely equipped, temporary bases. In these circumstances, the Joint Commander of deployed forces must be able to exercise effective control over his supply chain, which must in turn be flexible and capable of adjusting rapidly to changing front line priorities. We are therefore putting in place a Joint Force Logistic Component Headquarters as part of a joint headquarters to co-ordinate all joint logistics support.

40.   Elsewhere in the support area, there has been growing dependence on one Service providing support to the others on a joint basis. But there is much more we now need to do to ensure that the support areas can meet the changing demands of the front line.

41.   Fundamental to our approach is a radical restructuring of the whole organisation of logistic support to introduce much greater joint direction and management. The three single Service logistics organisations will be brought together into a unified structure to provide logistic support to all the Services. A Chief of Defence Logistics will be appointed to take control of the existing organisations and to reconfigure them into a single integrated organisation. This will take time to achieve but its advantages should be significant. It will encourage the greater interoperability of logistics systems, develop a pan-defence business overview and spread best practice throughout the support area. It will also help extend the benefits from the Smart Procurement initiative into the logistics field.

42.   Development of a properly integrated logistic structure will require other changes as well. This will be an evolutionary process which is set out in more detail in the essay on 'Support and Infrastrucure'. Among the first steps will be:

  – formation of transitional joint Defence Explosive and Non-explosive Storage and Distribution Agencies, which will be unified to perform all storage and distribution tasks from 2004/05;

  – the formation of a Joint Defence Transport and Movements organisation to take responsibility for the movement of all personnel and materiel;

  – formation of a single Defence Aircraft Repair Agency to repair and overhaul all military aircraft, both fixed-wing and helicopters;

  – centralisation of the procurement and management of fuels and lubricants across defence.

43.   The new joint organisation for defence logistics will strengthen our strategic logistics planning, matching logistics support more effectively to the requirements of joint operations. We will be able to implement innovative ideas throughout the support organisation more quickly and achieve closer integration of the supply network, particularly by the use of information technology. Industry will see consistent and coherent business processes in the logistics area, complementing the changes to be implemented under Smart Procurement. Modern forces need modern support. These initiatives will help provide it.

Conclusions

44.   The measures set out above are logical and important steps in the modernisation of our Armed Forces. By building on the successful joint initiatives already taken, we will ensure that we can deliver forces in support of Britain's foreign and security policy aims which together provide a greater capability than the sum of their individual parts.

45.   The realisation of the Joint Vision will be dependent on our personnel and their preparedness to think about defence in new ways. Feedback during the Review from all levels of the Services has confirmed that the need for effective tri-Service operational and support structures is recognised and welcomed where it makes sense operationally, and reflects experience and consultation rather than dogma. The changes we are introducing will reinforce the successes already achieved whilst retaining the individuality of the single Services which generate so much of the pride, loyalty and commitment of our people.

SUPPORTING ESSAY NINE
A POLICY FOR PEOPLE

INTRODUCTION

1.   To have modern and effective Armed Forces, we must recruit and retain our fair share of the best people the country has to offer. The quality of our people and their readiness for the tasks entrusted to them are the true measure of our Forces' operational capability. The skills and experience we have been able to give our personnel, Service and civilian, their capacity for innovation and their morale and motivation are fundamental to Britain's defence.

2.   We must therefore ensure that our personnel policies maintain our operational effectiveness and ensure that it is backed up, where necessary, by appropriate and demonstrable fighting power. Any change must be measured against this test. Our personnel policies need to match the best elsewhere to ensure that our people can give of their best.

3.   Because our people and their views are so important, a key part of the Strategic Defence Review (SDR) was to supplement the normal consultation processes to enable us to know for certain just what are the issues of real concern. To this end the Defence Secretary directed that a liaison team be formed to talk directly to Service and civilian staff to discuss with them the issues raised by the SDR, and listen, first hand, to their concerns and ideas. In a programme of over eighty visits the team (which comprised a member from each of the Services and two civil servants) talked with audiences totalling some 7,000 people. Examples of what people had to say are reproduced throughout this essay including all the quotations. We are committed, through our Policy for People, to address the issues they raised.

4.   Our Policy for People does not just include initiatives which have arisen out of the Review but incorporates others already in hand and those planned for the future to produce a coherent and comprehensive programme. On the Service side, we have endorsed the considerable work that was already in progress following the *Independent Review of the Armed Forces' Manpower, Career and Remuneration Structures, (HMSO 1995)* and the 1997 information document *The Armed Forces of The Future – A Personnel Strategy,* upon which we have drawn for our Policy for People.

5.   Despite this we have, however, concluded that we need to do more. We are determined to have terms and conditions of service which are both relevant to the 21st century and balance the needs of the individual with those of the organisation. On the civilian side, we will continue to build on our Personnel Policy Statement and our Civilian Personnel Management Strategy *Personnel Policy Statement for Civil Servants Employed in the Ministry of Defence (September 1995)* and *Civilian Personnel Management Strategy: An Agenda for the next Two Years, (August 1997)*.

6.   We must be a modern and fair employer. We have pledged ourselves to continuous improvement in all our practices. For instance, we are implementing one of the biggest and most demanding Investors in People (IiP) programmes in the Country. Achieving IiP accreditation will help us to ensure that all personnel are properly trained and developed to meet our goals and targets, and that our significant investment in development and training, some £1Bn a year, is properly targetted and evaluated.

7.   We are also committed to making real progress on improving our record on equal opportunities through tackling the complex web of underlying factors which have inhibited people from various backgrounds choosing to join us in the past. We must ensure that those who join us make progress according to their talents and legitimate aspirations.

8.   Our Policy for People balances the needs of the MOD and our staff and, wherever possible, responds to the legitimate concerns expressed recently during the consultation process by Service and civilian personnel, trade unions and outside commentators. Our conclusions, plans and proposals are set out below.

SERVICE PERSONNEL

Current Concerns

"If we don't look at personnel issues then the SDR will fail."

(Note: This and all other quotations are statements made to the Strategic Defence Review Liaison Team. In order to preserve confidentiality they have not been attributed to individuals).

9.   **Overstretch and Undermanning.** We know there are problems. Two of the most intractable, overstretch and undermanning, have existed for years and are themselves manifestations of deeper problems. The Armed Forces know they cannot be solved overnight and they would be suspicious of anyone who claimed otherwise. They also understand that personnel policy alone cannot resolve the imbalances between wider Defence Policy, commitments and resources. It must be part of a whole but, if we do not have a magic wand, we do have a determination to get things done. If some of the proposals in our Policy for People seem modest it is only because we have promised what we can deliver. Addressing the personnel problems that affect the Armed Forces will take time, trust, and money. Trust needs to be earned and will only arise from the delivery of tangible improvements in overstretch and undermanning.

"We are continually away from our families – there is no incentive to stay."

10.   **Unit Overstretch.** Some of the causes of unit overstretch (too few units to meet commitments) are avoidable. So we have decided, as described elsewhere, to address the causes to ensure that there is a much better balance between resources and commitments. Specifically in the Royal Navy we have reduced the peacetime tasking required from the destroyer, frigate and submarine forces. In the Army, we will maintain our current level of commitments but increase establishments by 3,300 personnel and create a sixth deployable brigade. The size of Royal Air Force front line has been set against the level of commitment we expect it to meet. Extra logistic and medical units will be formed for all three Services and, as they become fully manned, will relieve overstretch in some of the most hard pressed areas. These measures are described in detail in other essays. It will take time for them to produce results but we are determined to put them in place as quickly as possible.

"Constant commitments are stopping people from training properly and developing their careers – so they leave early."

11.   **Individual Overstretch.** For a large number of Service personnel the effects of unit overstretch are exacerbated by undermanning, which together cause individual overstretch. At present we do not have enough information to determine the size of individual overstretch or to identify solutions. All three Services are looking to remedy this. The Royal Air Force has developed a technique to record separated service. The Royal Navy and the Army are looking to adopt a similar system to ensure that individual overstretch and turbulence are managed as equitably as possible. In the meantime, the measures we are introducing to alleviate unit overstretch should also lead to reductions in individual overstretch. Matching resources to commitments will reduce turbulence and bring some stability back into people's lives.

"Manning is getting worse and we cannot see that the SDR will change anything."

12.   **Undermanning.** The effects of undermanning are obvious, the causes many. At its simplest it happens because we neither recruit sufficient numbers nor retain Service personnel for long enough. This has caused a vicious circle to ensue, where undermanning causes individual overstretch, itself a function of unit overstretch, which then causes further undermanning and so on. This will be a difficult circle to break, but we intend so to do.

13.   **Breaking the Circle.** We intend to break the circle by removing unit overstretch and achieving full manning (through improving recruiting and retention) so that we can reduce individual overstretch to manageable proportions. We expect largely to remove unit overstretch once we reach full manning. If we are successful, full manning in the Royal Air Force should be achieved by 2000, the Royal Navy by 2002 and the Army around 2004. The increase in the Army establishment described above is the main reason why it will take longer to reach full manning. Once reached this will have a significant impact, for the better, on individual overstretch.

14.   To maintain proper, balanced career structures, we may not be able to achieve full manning without some redundancy in a limited number of employment categories. This will not be on the scale of previous programmes. There may be about 200 redundancies in the Royal Navy as a whole, targeting certain specialist categories and on a voluntary basis. No redundancies are envisaged in the Army or the Royal Air Force.

15.   **Improving Recruiting and Retention.** The issues most frequently recorded by the SDR liaison team which would improve recruiting and retention included better terms and conditions of service, improvements in pay and allowances, better quality of training, reducing overstretch, allowing service beyond 22 years, providing opportunities to gain civilian qualifications during service, addressing concerns about family life, ensuring equality of opportunity and providing better accommodation. Other evidence from recent leavers' surveys showed that reducing separation from family and friends and improving promotion prospects would also be important.

16.   All of these suggestions have been considered carefully and have been used to develop a package of measures, building on much that was already being done, to help the individual and the family, both in the short and long term, and which we believe will improve recruiting and retention.

Improvement Plans – Strategy For The 21st Century

"We need a vision for the future."

17.   To provide a framework for addressing the problems we have identified, we need a comprehensive personnel strategy to take the Armed Forces into the next century. It must:
  - incorporate all that is best in current practice, build upon the important work already in hand and respect the traditions of the three individual Services, especially the ethos and values needed to support operational capability;
  - provide jobs which are rewarding and challenging;
  - allow us to recruit, retain and motivate the people we need by offering pay, allowances and a pension scheme broadly comparable to those in the civilian sector, but which recognise the demands of service life and the role of the Armed Forces Pay Review Body;
  - enable individuals to realise their full potential during their service, provide equality of opportunity irrespective of race, gender or religion, and assist them to prepare for subsequent careers;
  - manage postings so that the operational requirement is met, but take individual aspirations for family stability into account as far as practicable.

Underpinning our strategy will be measures to improve recruiting, retention and resettlement. Critical to success will be measures to reduce overstretch and undermanning. These, however, will take time to have the effect we want.

18.   We will therefore proceed with other measures whose effect on the individual and Service family will be more immediate. To improve recruiting we will continue with our measures to embrace all sections of the community, irrespective of gender or race and we will improve the provision for education and training on joining and within the Services. This will re-emphasise the value of a career of first choice in the Forces.

19.   We also aim to improve retention with a range of new measures including: enhancements to operational welfare, introduction of a common leave entitlement and a programme to improve standards of single living accommodation.

20.   We intend to address the concerns of Service families. As a first step we will establish a families task force. We will also ensure that the already high quality of education delivered by the Service Children's Education Agency is enhanced even further.

21.   We intend to introduce a career transition service and, in a major initiative, we will improve aftercare provision with the establishment of a veterans' advice cell.

Improvement Plans – For The Individual

'LEARNING FORCES' – IMPROVED PROVISION FOR EDUCATION AND TRAINING

"To improve recruiting, give the potential Serviceman at the Recruiting Office a definite lead on his career and what qualifications he may attain."

22.   Our consultation process reinforced our view that the perceived lack of opportunities to gain recognised civilian qualifications discouraged potential recruits from joining and caused Service personnel to leave prematurely. Within the framework of the Government's 'Learning Age' proposals, our 'Learning Forces' initiative will introduce a range of measures for the provision of better opportunities for personal development linked to academic, vocational and professional qualifications. We will provide substantial additional resources to fund these initiatives, based on the following principles:

- competence in key skills, related to national targets and rank/employment;
- the opportunity to gain recognised and transferable qualifications;
- funding for learning activities during and after service;
- provision of Personal Development Records;
- access to information, advice and modern learning facilities, irrespective of rank, age, employment or location;
- return the individual to the civilian workplace with "added value".

23.   **Key Skills.** We will take action to ensure that all recruits will have an opportunity to gain an appropriate level of competence in the six key skills identified by Department for Education and Employment (DfEE) as needed by all in the workplace. Those skills include competence in literacy, numeracy and information technology. From 2000, some 1,300 school leavers a year will also have the opportunity to attend the new Army Foundation College for a 43 week course which will offer a National Traineeship and a Level 2 Scottish/National Vocational Qualification which will include Level 2 Key Skills commensurate with the ability of the student.

Recognised and Transferable Qualifications

"There is a need for civilian recognised qualifications."

24.   **Scottish/National Vocational Qualifications (S/NVQs).** We recognise the considerable recruitment, retention and resettlement benefits of providing civilian recognised and transferable training for our military and civilian personnel, particularly S/NVQs. We wish to ensure that all military trade and professional training that can gain civilian recognition and formal accreditation does so. Most technical training within the Armed Forces already attracts civilian qualifications. We estimate that up to 70% of all training within the Armed Forces could be so eligible.

25.   **S/NVQ Level 2.** For the purposes of illustration, S/NVQ Level 2 is the broad equivalent of the academic attainment of achieving five GCSEs. Additional resources will be provided to give all non commissioned service personnel the opportunity to gain an S/NVQ Level 2 within three years, or by the time they complete their minimum engagement, whichever is the later.

Learning Credits

"We need to offer more in-Service education to retain people."

26.   We will expand education and vocational training opportunities for the Armed Forces. Service personnel will be able to claim 'Learning Credits' for education and vocational training both while serving and for some time afterwards. When the DfEE Individual Learning Accounts are established we will, if necessary, adjust our proposals more closely to reflect them. We believe that it is right to retain an individual contribution to these schemes.

Personal Development Record

27.   All military personnel will be provided with a Personal Development Record (PDR), to be retained throughout their Service career. That, in line with the DfEE Learning Age proposals, will be used to record the experience and qualifications they gain and provide opportunities to signpost routes/means for further development. It will be tangible proof for a prospective employer of their record of achievement and aspirations. The introduction of PDRs will be supported by a developing structure for accreditation of military education, training and experience in terms of national credit ratings.

IMPROVED SINGLE LIVING ACCOMMODATION

"Junior accommodation has been neglected and is in a bad state."

28.   The strategy for improvements in the service families estate have not been matched by a similar strategy for improvements in single living accommodation. The SDR Liaison Team found sub-standard single accommodation to be a significant area of complaint. The Armed Forces Pay Review Body has consistently criticised the low priority this has been given in the past.

29.   In future, new accommodation will be built so that, in most instances, individuals of all ranks will be provided with a single room. There are plans in place now to raise the standard of some existing single living accommodation, and we have initiated a survey of all single living accommodation to inform our longer term aspiration to improve the whole estate.

OPERATIONAL WELFARE ENHANCEMENTS

"Welfare is key."

30.   The provision of welfare support for Service and civilian personnel deployed on operations is a key component in the maintenance of morale and thus the overall effectiveness of deployed forces. Small enhancements in this area can cause a disproportionate increase in morale. Although much is already done, we have recognised that in two areas - the financial assistance provided for telephone calls home and the provision of Rest and Recuperation flights – more is needed.

Telephone Calls. Personnel deployed on operations in for example Bosnia and the Gulf are currently entitled to financial support for welfare telephone calls roughly equating to a three minute call a week. That is too short for a satisfactory family call, particularly where young children are involved. We will increase the time for entitled personnel to ten minutes. We are investigating extending this provision to personnel on operational ships dependent on telephone facilities being available and operational feasibility.

Additional Rest and Recuperation Flights. Our experience in Bosnia has shown that a small proportion of Service personnel may be deployed for eleven months or more. Those personnel are currently eligible for two rest and recuperation flights. We will increase the number of flights for such personnel to three. For those deployed for longer than 13 months, additional flights will be provided.

Satellite TV on Royal Navy Ships. We are exploring extending the provision of satellite TV to all Royal Navy ships whilst at sea. It is currently installed on our aircraft carriers where it has been an important factor in contributing to morale, particularly on prolonged deployments. There are, however, technical difficulties in extending it to the rest of the Fleet and work is in hand to determine whether our aspirations can be realised.

31.   **Allowances.** Enhancements to operational welfare need to be seen within the context of the 1995 Independent Review. An updated allowance package, based on its recommendations, was introduced last year. This was targeted at aligning allowances more closely to our current operational stance. It included a longer separated service allowance for those on long or frequent periods on operations, exercise and training away from their base and a get you home allowance which provides a contribution to the cost of travelling home for those on detached duty or courses. We will monitor the effectiveness of these allowances to confirm they are having the consequences we intended.

LEAVE ENTITLEMENT

32.   The Services do not currently have a common annual leave allowance. Junior ranks in the Army and Royal Air Force, serving in the United Kingdom and the rest of the world, less North West Europe, are allowed less than senior ranks and officers. We therefore intend that, from April 1999, all ranks of all three Services should move to a common leave allowance of 30 'working days'. For this purpose the 'working days' of the week are Monday to Friday.

NEW CAREER TRANSITION SERVICE

33.   We will improve current resettlement provision. This autumn we intend to introduce the Career Transition Partnership, in conjunction with a private sector supplier. For leavers with over five years' service, it will provide career transition support, including unlimited counselling, workshops and nationwide job finding support. At the same time, we will introduce enhanced job finding support for those with between three and five years' service. Our marketing campaign "Access to Excellence" will continue as will all current single Service resettlement support. We will also introduce, from April 1999, a graduated resettlement scheme. This will make available increased time, up to a maximum of seven weeks, linked to length of service, for career transition preparation. Our overall intention is to ensure that Service leavers receive the best preparation for their future careers.

VETERANS' ADVICE CELL

"SDR should be looking to improve the welfare support organisations."

34.   Ex-Service personnel and Service charities made us aware that there is no single point of contact which ex-Service personnel can approach so that they can be directed to those best able to deal with their particular problems. We will remedy this with the establishment of a Veterans' Advice Cell. This will be staffed

by Service or ex-Service personnel who can provide guidance on where and how to obtain specific expert assistance. The Veterans' Advice Cell will also enable us to identify quickly any changing welfare requirements for veterans by monitoring the type and frequency of the requests that are made. That will enable us to identify and address issues before they become major problems. We plan to have the Cell operational, within the MOD, later this year.

Improvement Plans – For The Family

"To have an effective review you need to canvas the views of our wives."

35. **Service Families Task Force.** We are keenly aware of the problems that Service life can pose for families. "Following the Flag" means that spouses will invariably have to give up their jobs in circumstances which render them ineligible for the Job Seekers' Allowance, will have to find places for their children in suitable schools, register with a doctor and struggle to find an NHS dentist. That is an exhausting but not exhaustive list – additional problems occur over social security allowances and access to some NHS treatments. We intend to establish a task force to address the concerns of Service families. This will take time but we are determined to drive it forward.

ENHANCEMENT TO PROVISION FOR SERVICE CHILDREN'S EDUCATION

36. Service personnel are concerned that their children are not disadvantaged as a result of their service overseas. The majority of Service children overseas attend schools maintained by the Service Children's Education (SCE) Agency. We intend in SCE to mirror the initiatives announced by the DfEE during the past year including the literacy and numeracy projects, improvements to school security (for example, to provide school fencing for those without) and training for School Advisory Committee members. Increased funding for these initiatives will be provided.

37. Those measures are in addition to the funds already allocated to replicate the provision of nursery education in civilian schools for all four year olds. Under this scheme, and in locations where there is already an SCE school or garrison playgroup, the facilities will be extended to cater for all four year olds with effect from September 1998, and sooner in some areas. In overseas locations where there is no integral SCE provision, or where numbers are insufficient to create a viable nursery class or pre-school group, Service parents will be given financial assistance to offset the costs of sending their children to a local nursery school.

Improvement Plans – Personnel Management

EQUAL OPPORTUNITIES

"Will SDR comment on discrimination?"

38. **Equal Opportunity Training.** A Tri-Service Equal Opportunities Training Centre has been established at Shrivenham. Its purpose is to provide comprehensive training to Service Equal Opportunity Advisers, trainers and senior officers (i.e. Brigadiers or equivalent and above). All officers at brigadier level or equivalent are to receive mandatory equal opportunities training which will emphasise their leadership responsibility in this crucial area. All recruiting staff, new recruits, NCOs, junior officers and commanding officers now receive equal opportunities training.

39. **Women.** The three Services are wholly committed to maximising opportunity for women in the Armed Forces, except where this would damage combat effectiveness. 96% of posts in the Royal Air Force and 73% of the total posts in the Royal Navy and Royal Marines have been open to women for some time. On 1 April 1998, the Army increased the posts open to women from 47% to 70%. We have been reviewing whether we could improve the opportunities still further. As a result, we have decided that some 1300 posts in Army and Navy specialist units attached to the Royal Marines will be open to women. We have, however, concluded that posts in the Royal Marines, the RAF Regiment and those in the Army whose primary role in battle is to "close with and kill the enemy" should remain closed to women until we can properly assess, in two to three years, the impact on combat effectiveness of the recently introduced changes in the Army. Women are also currently excluded from service on submarines and as Royal Navy mine clearance divers for medical or practical reasons. Reviews of these areas will be completed towards the end of this year.

40. Servicewomen currently represent around 7% of the total strength of the Armed Forces. More women are joining the Forces and fewer are leaving. In the last year 14% of all new recruits were women and there was a 30% decrease in the numbers leaving. We hope that the numbers of recruits will increase, particularly as the Army has specifically targeted women in its most recent recruiting campaign. Additional work is also under way to establish a system of monitoring gender related issues including recruiting and maternity related aspects, building on experience gained from the ethnic monitoring programme. That will provide us with objective evidence of our success, or otherwise, on gender issues.

41. **Ethnic Minorities.** We are determined that the Armed Forces should better reflect the ethnic composition of the British population. Currently some 6% of the general population are from ethnic minority backgrounds, but they make up just 1% of the Services. This must not continue. We have set a goal of attracting 2% of new recruits this year from ethnic minority communities for each Service. We want that goal to increase by 1% each year so that, eventually, the composition of our Armed Forces reflects that of the population as a whole.

42. To encourage more members of the ethnic minorities to join the Armed Forces, and stay in once they have joined, we have been working hard to accommodate religious and cultural differences such as dress and diet wherever possible, while still maintaining combat effectiveness. We are working to develop and increase outreach work with local communities. We will continue to work closely in partnership with the Commission for Racial Equality (CRE), to persist with our efforts in the recruitment of ethnic minorities and to combat racism. We were delighted that earlier this year the CRE agreed to lift the threat of legal action against the Department and replace it by a partnership agreement between the MOD and the Commission. The Chairman of the CRE described this as, "A model of leadership in action". All three Services achieved a modest improvement in recruitment in 1997/98. We have introduced a further range of measures including ethnic minorities recruiting teams. There is a long way to go but we are fully committed to achieving this goal.

43. **Harassment.** All personnel have the right to work without fear of harassment or bullying. We have made clear our policy of zero tolerance on harassment. Any form of harassment is completely contrary to the military ethos; it is unacceptable and will not be tolerated. That is made explicit in directives promulgated by each of the three Services. We are determined that the principles laid down in those directives will be followed by all and that appropriate action will be taken where this does not occur.

44. **Confidential Support Telephone Lines.** Our policy of zero tolerance is not new. Confidential support telephone lines have been introduced (although they may not always be accessible from ships at sea) to offer completely confidential guidance across the whole range of personnel matters. They also allow personnel to seek advice on how to deal with harassment. Support lines do not undermine the individual chain of command arrangements for complaints, which remain in place.

Improvement Plans – Longer Term Initiatives

DEVELOP A COMMON OVERARCHING PERSONNEL STRATEGY

45.   One of the key recommendations of the Independent Review for the improvement of personnel policy was that the MOD should develop an overall strategic personnel policy and then ensure that each Service developed its own sub-strategy, policies and practices relevant to its own needs. This is a recommendation we wish to see implemented. We will produce an overarching personnel strategy with an associated action plan clearly identifying specific MOD and Service responsibilities. The Services are producing their own human resources strategies which will be linked into the overall strategy.

46.   The introduction of a common personnel strategy will require care. The Independent Review recognised that some employment conditions needed to be common and some to be different. Those differences that must remain to preserve operational effectiveness will be kept; those that are not will be harmonised. The introduction of such a strategy should result in an increase in operational effectiveness, avoiding the difficulties which can occur on joint operations because of unnecessary single Service differences. We intend to introduce best practice across all three Services and secure administrative benefits through the use of common and standardised procedures. We will not, however, undermine the individual identity or ethos of each Service, but will recognise the contribution all three Services make to the provision of overall defence capability.

BETTER CAREER MANAGEMENT

47.   The Independent Review recognised that all Service personnel were required to be mobile, that Service commanders rarely had the opportunity to select those personnel posted to them and that, accordingly, the quality and reliability of central personnel management in each of the Services was unusually important. We will continue to pursue improvements in postings policy and in career management. In an era of increasing openness, we wish to encourage a greater contribution by the individual in the development of his/her career in active liaison with career managers, so that the individual has the opportunity to fulfil his/her full potential.

48.   **Common Appraisal System.** We need a consistent approach across all three Services to evaluation and proper assessment of performance against objectives. Although the Royal Navy and Royal Air Force have just introduced new appraisal systems, we have recognised the further advantages to be gained from having a common system across the Armed Forces. The Services have now decided to adopt an essentially common appraisal system for all commissioned officers. The new, common system will continue to provide feedback on performance and assist processes for identifying candidates for promotion, appointments and further training. In addition, it will be as simple and un-bureaucratic as possible and comply with the requirements of IiP. We aim to introduce the system in the year 2000.

49.   **Career Structures.** Significant work has already been done in all three Services to develop future officer and non commissioned career structures, informed by the recommendations of the Independent Review, to take account of trends in the wider workplace. We are considering how to make better use of the experience of the non-commissioned other ranks. We would like to maximise the already substantial transfer that currently takes place through later commissioning - between 20-30% of the Officer Corps in all three Services is made up of late entry commissions or commissions from the ranks.

DEVELOP AN OVERARCHING RECRUITING STRATEGY

"We must attend to recruiting problems now, as we are overstretched."

50.   We need an overarching recruiting strategy to get best value out of the almost £100M we spend each year on recruiting. This strategy must co-ordinate more closely our current recruiting effort and spread best practice. We need to ensure that sufficient numbers of young people of the required calibre are attracted to a career in the Services so that the correct balance of age, skills and expertise can be maintained within both our regular and reserve Forces. Failure would lead to a loss of operational capability.

51.   We must therefore ensure that the role of the Armed Forces in the 21st century and the attractions of a Service career are widely understood across the whole community, hence the importance we attach to our initiatives on lifelong learning and equal opportunities. Our strategy will:

- emphasise the rewarding and challenging career opportunities within the Services (including the opportunity for all to gain recognised civilian qualifications);

- provide effective enquiry and recruiting arrangements, and will ensure that all applications are processed fairly and properly;

- provide a focus for all recruiting activity while maintaining the image of the three single Services – we recognise that potential recruits will want to join "the Navy", not "Defence".

INTRODUCE NEW PAY SYSTEM

"Pay is fundamental to the SDR otherwise we will lose our expertise."

52.   Since 1971 the level of Service pay has reflected the recommendations of the Armed Forces Pay Review Body (AFPRB). Throughout the consultation process we were told that the current pay structure was inadequate to meet the future needs of the Armed Services. We share the view of the AFPRB that there is a need for a new system. We have endorsed the work which was already in hand to introduce a new pay structure whereby an individual's pay will increase within a rank in accordance with specified criteria; i.e. experience, professional qualifications and satisfactory performance. We hope to have this established by 1 April 2000.

53.   Additional pay will continue to be paid to respond to the recruiting and retention needs in specialist skill groups. Evidence is being prepared for the AFPRB's consideration for a simple, flexible and better system.

INTRODUCE PAY AS YOU DINE

54.   Currently Service personnel occupying single living accommodation pay a daily food charge, irrespective of whether or not they actually consume the meals provided. Many Service personnel feel this is unfair. The Independent Review recommended the earliest practicable introduction (with the exception, notably, of catering services in the field and in ships) of a system enabling military personnel to pay only for those meals or items actually consumed. That is Pay As You Dine (PAYD). Work is underway to determine the Armed Forces' requirements and the full implications for the MOD before preparing a request for proposals from a commercial partner. We envisage a commercial partner would be able to enhance dining facilities (particularly for Junior Ranks), and provide a range of new services such as take away or home delivery.

REVIEW COMPENSATION AND PENSION ARRANGEMENTS

"A person who loses a limb whilst serving his country gets no recompense."

55.   **Compensation Arrangements.** Concerns have been expressed about current arrangements to compensate Service personnel for injury, illness and death. These must reflect modern standards and be consistent with the legitimate expectations of Service men and women. A review of the principles underlying a possible new structure of compensation is underway. We wish to establish clear criteria for determining eligibility for awards and to set benefits at levels which are fair to individuals and consistent with good practice elsewhere. A consultation document will be issued.

56.   **Armed Forces' Pensions Scheme.** We also intend to review the Armed Forces Pension Scheme, taking into account the arrangements for the provision of pensions in the public sector and elsewhere. Our objective will be to introduce arrangements which will meet the future manning needs of the Armed Forces in a way that is fair, cost-effective and affordable.

MILITARY DISCIPLINE AND JUSTICE

57.   A military system of justice which reflects the unique circumstances within the Armed Forces is vital: but the system must remain up to date and command respect within the Services and more widely. Reforms in the court martial system have been introduced to increase the independence and perceived impartiality of the courts and streamline their operation.

58.   **Tri-Service Discipline Act.** We believe there would be advantages to be gained from combining the three Service Discipline Acts into a single Act. Those differences which the Services need to retain for operational reasons would be kept but reduced to the absolute minimum. That would require a complete rewrite of the legislation but would allow the Services to define their needs for the next millennium and translate them into legislation where necessary. That would be a substantial and complex undertaking which will take some years to complete, but one which we consider would be very worthwhile.

59.   **Membership of Courts Martial.** In recognition of the value of Warrant Officers and their experience in contributing to the administration of justice, the Services will amend the eligibility criteria for membership of Courts Martial to allow Warrant Officers to sit as members of the panel where sergeants and more junior ranks (or equivalent) have been arraigned. This change requires legislation and it will be included in the next Armed Forces Bill in 2001.

Key Points – Service Personnel

For the Individual

- Lifelong Learning – all recruits to have the opportunity for personal development whilst serving and to gain civilian qualifications. Help for all personnel to pursue personal development and gain civilian qualifications during and after their service. As much service experience and as many courses will, as far as possible, be externally accredited to attract valid civilian qualifications.
- Better Single Living Accommodation.
- Improved Operational Welfare.
- Standard Leave Entitlements Irrespective of Rank.
- New Career Transition Support Service.
- Veterans' Advice Cell.

For the Family

- Establish a Service Families Task Force.

- Enhancements to Provision for Service Children's Education.

Personnel Management

Equal Opportunities – maximise our efforts to recruit the very best, irrespective of gender, religious, ethnic or social background. Continue our efforts to make a Service career attractive to all.

Longer Term Initiatives

- Introduce an Overarching Personnel Strategy.

- Introduce an Overarching Recruiting Strategy.

- Better Career Management - common appraisal for commissioned officers.

- New Pay System.

- Review Compensation and Pension Arrangements.

- Pay As You Dine.

- Military Discipline and Justice – changes to membership of some Courts Martial, review of tri-Service Discipline Act.

CIVILIAN STAFF

Current Concerns

"Civilian staff feel that they don't matter."

60.   Civilian staff in the MOD make a key contribution to our Defence effort. They undertake many crucial tasks in support of the Services and in some cases work alongside them on operations.

61.   Nevertheless, many have felt that they have been undervalued over the last few years. There have been major organisational changes, people have been transferred to private sector employers, have had to move homes when work has been relocated and have faced changed expectations and management arrangements because of decentralisation and delegation. The cumulative effect has been to make people more uncertain about their future careers while at the same time requiring them to cope with 'initiative overload.'

62.   It will never be right to put a stop to change. The MOD, like all employers, will continue to improve its performance and adapt to changing circumstances and operational imperatives. However, there is now increasing commitment to policies for civilian staff more attuned to the real needs of people who work for the Department and their families. There is a new focus on promoting excellence in the management of civilian staff, explaining and putting into practice good intentions which may have been expressed in the past but sometimes not properly implemented or given time to take root.

"Everything seems ad hoc, with no overall plan."

63.   Our principles for the management of our civilian staff have been set out in our Civilian Personnel Management Strategy *Civilian Personnel Management Strategy: An Agenda for the Next Two Years;* and in the Personnel Policy Statement. *Personnel Policy Statement for Civil Servants Employed in the Ministry of Defence:*

- all staff in delegated management units and Agencies remain employees of the MOD, with opportunities across the Department and managed according to common principles of good management;

- MOD is an equal opportunities employer;

- MOD is committed to the Civil Service principles of recruitment on merit through fair and open competition, and promotion on merit;

- MOD will continue to invest in the training and development of staff to enable all to make a full contribution and enhance their potential;

- staff will be equipped with the skills, knowledge and awareness they need and will receive the clear and timely information which they need to do their jobs.

Source: MOD publications, 1995 and 1997

64.   Those principles have been underpinned by a wide range of practical measures which aim to preserve the benefits for managers and staff of working in a large and diverse organisation, but give units and individuals more scope to develop skills and careers in ways which best suit them.

CAREER MANAGEMENT

"Some managers don't seem to care about people's careers any more – you're on your own now."

65.   Over the last few years, the Department has seen important new systems for civilian management put into place which provide a framework matching best practice in other departments and the private sector. "Competence frameworks" help people identify the skills and experience they need. Revised appraisal systems help people be clear about the key purpose of their jobs, their objectives, and how they are expected to perform and develop. Annual training and development plans are produced and reviewed for individuals and business units. Assessment centres are used for promotions to the key management level below the Senior Civil Service. There is a mixed economy of job advertising and managed job changes to encourage a partnership between individuals, line managers and personnel managers in reconciling the aspirations of individuals and the needs of the Department.

Improvement Plans

66.   Against this background, we have identified several areas for additional priority action:

- clearer career information and guidance;

- greater encouragement for continuous professional development;

- active promotion of practical equal opportunities measures and training which make a difference;

- reduced central regulation and more responsive flexible systems;

- better upward and downward communication.

    Source: Civilian Personnel Management Strategy: An Agenda for the Next Two Years, (1997)

CAREER GUIDANCE

67.   We have already published Planning for Your Future *Planning for Your Future: a Guide to Career Development in the Ministry of Defence (November 1997)*, a manual of career development guidance which gives examples of the types of opportunities available and guidance on how to assess options. That is just the beginning and further guidance and support arrangements are being developed centrally and in management units.

LIFELONG LEARNING

68.   We are determined to encourage lifelong learning. We have increased investment in a range of focused training and development programmes and improved infrastructure for training delivery. We have introduced systems through which people's training and broader development needs are kept under regular review. We have in place the full range of schemes to support day release, adult further education and external training programmes, and we are committed to expanding our involvement in interchange and volunteering programmes with links to the community at large, such as those run by the Prince's Trust.

69.   To develop greater professionalism, support is being extended to an increasing number of staff studying for professional qualifications, including MBAs. Much improved arrangements and incentives for professional finance training are in place and we are considering similar measures for other functions. A number of schemes have been developed to help people achieve S/NVQs. These are being expanded. The MOD's modern apprentice scheme for industrial staff, a widely regarded model of its kind, now attracts almost 300 apprentices a year. A wide range of modules is increasingly being provided through information technology based inter-active learning packages available at an increasing number of new interactive learning facilities (ILFs) across the UK and in overseas locations.

INVESTORS IN PEOPLE

70.   It is fundamental that the policies and initiatives outlined above deliver results. Our commitment to the Investors in People (IiP) standards and process will be an additional spur to ensure that that happens. Throughout the Department the managers of individual units and their staff are committed to tackle by the year 2000 the gaps they have identified between fine words and best practice. IiP assessments will provide a widely respected rigorous independent check.

Equal opportunities

71.   For several years we have placed a high priority on carrying out equal opportunities programmes to enhance the position of minority groups amongst our civilian staff. While some progress has been made, we are completely committed to improving equal opportunities:

  – all line managers of civilian staff in the Department – Service and Civilian – will undergo appropriate equal opportunities training over the next three two years;

  – action plans are being developed targeting equal opportunity measures for women, the disabled and ethnic minority staff;

  – all personnel management policies and procedures have been reviewed to check that they conform with the requirements of the Disability Discrimination Act;

- we have nursery arrangements in an increasing number of locations, and are keen to continue to develop family friendly policies through flexible working and other means;

- we continue to operate harassment helplines for staff in need;

- we will implement the Working Time Directive to ensure that unreasonable demands are not made on people to work excessive hours;

- in monitoring our recruitment of civilian staff from different ethnic backgrounds, we will in future assess progress according to the composition of relevant employment catchment areas. We will pay particular attention to those areas where action is likely to be most needed and most effective.

PAY, GRADING AND CONDITIONS OF SERVICE

"Pay and grading arrangements are too complicated."

72. Important steps are being taken to improve pay and grading arrangements by removing unnecessary complexity whilst providing greater flexibility for managers and staff, yet retaining fair and equitable structures. Improved and simpler performance pay arrangements were introduced last year for most non-industrial staff and a programme of further changes for both industrial and non-industrial staff is under discussion with the trades unions. We wish to see the terms and conditions of both groups of staff brought into line, wherever this makes sense and meets Departmental and staff needs, and thus move towards the concept of a single status workforce for all of our civilian employees.

"Conditions of service and working conditions do not match those of good outside employers."

73. We are determined that our staff should have a package of terms and conditions which match good practice elsewhere and meet modern expectations. Entitlements to annual, maternity and paternity leave are being improved, and work is in progress to develop an improved pension scheme which will be introduced throughout the Civil Service early in the new millennium.

74. We will also continue to make improvements to the working environment for our staff as has been achieved successfully and cost effectively in the Defence Evaluation and Research Agency at Farnborough and at the Procurement Executive complex at Abbey Wood in Bristol. The proposed redevelopment project for the Main Building will be taken forward on the same basis.

REORGANISATION AND TRANSFER OF WORK

"We are constantly being reorganised."

75. When issues about reorganisation or transfer of work arise, decisions are not being made because of dogma or the latest management theory. An informed pragmatic approach is now being taken, in consultation with staff and their trade union representatives, and the consequences for people, are being properly weighed and evaluated. We have learned a great deal from the extensive Competing for Quality (CFQ) programme. It has enabled the MOD to gain greater value for money from its limited budget. But, we are conscious of our duty of care to our loyal staff and are committed to looking after the interests of those affected by change in this way. To this end, we are introducing a Code of Practice for Transfer of Undertakings (Protection of Employment) (TUPE) agreed with trades unions and Industry which will ensure that the fullest attention is given to staff matters where personnel are transferred from the Civil Service.

CONSULTATION

"Top management does not listen."

76.   We will ensure that the views and opinions of our staff are sought, heard and taken into account as policies are developed and implemented. We will use the well-established procedures for consultation with staff and their trades union representatives on changes which have an effect on civilian staff interests. The constructive approach of staff and unions has been a crucial factor in helping produce major annual efficiency gains, and the procedures have served us well as the MOD has undergone the massive and widespread programme of reorganisation, relocation and reductions of the past few years.

77.   Those consultation procedures are being modernised and developed, and will continue to be supplemented by the kind of surveys, formal and informal, and direct consultation with staff which have been so welcomed during SDR. Timely upward feedback, and consultation and negotiation with the trades unions as appropriate, will remain a key way of ensuring that our policy for people is properly and practically focused and brings real results. Our IiP initiatives will be helpful here.

CONSEQUENCES OF SDR IMPLEMENTATION

78.   Consultation will be particularly important as the SDR is implemented and we take steps to ensure that the MOD continues to match the standards of a caring employer to which we are committed. There are likely to be three key areas of concern to staff:

-   **Relocation.** A comprehensive relocation package of compensation and practical assistance, which matches best practice in the private sector, is in place to ensure that when people and their families move home and job the stress is minimised.

-   **Early Departure and Redundancy.** Further major reductions of civilian staff are not required as a result of the SDR, but the current assessment is that in addition to plans previously announced a total of approximately another 1,400 posts are likely to be abolished over the next few years. Consequential staff reductions are likely to be considerably less and will be handled with full consultation and, as far as possible, through normal retirements and departures and adjustments to recruitment. Compulsory redundancy will be kept to the absolute minimum; appropriate compensation terms will be available, and professional outplacement services will be provided.

-   **Service in Operational Theatres.** Arrangements are in place to compensate for the difficulties and hardships of deployment to operational theatres such as Bosnia. These are designed to be broadly consistent with those for Service personnel and will be updated as necessary to meet new needs.

OVERALL OUTCOMES AND KEY SUCCESS CRITERIA

79.   The key test for our strategy and action plans for civilians, like the corresponding plans for the Services, is whether the fine words actually deliver practical common sense results and meet the legitimate aspirations which staff have expressed. We are determined to ensure that our Policy for People does just that over the next few years. Civilians, like their Service colleagues, deserve nothing less.

Key Points – Civilian Staff

Career Management, Training and Development

- Revised appraisal systems
- Better career guidance
- Investment in training and development
- Interactive learning facilities
- More interchange and voluntary programmes
- Support for MBAs, professional qualifications and S/NVQs
- Commitment to lifelong learning

Equal Opportunities

- Action plans for women, ethnic minority staff and those with disabilities
- Appropriate training for line managers – Service and civilian
- Nursery facilities increased
- Family friendly policies including flexible working

Pay and Conditions

- Simpler pay arrangements
- Proposals for streamlined grading arrangements
- Aim to bring industrial and non-industrial terms and conditions in line where appropriate

Investors in People

- Gap between departmental practice and IiP standard will be bridged
- Rigorous independent assessment

Reorganisation and Transfer of Work

- Approach based on pragmatism and value for money not dogma
- Code of Practice for any staff transferred from the Civil Service

Consultation

- Commitment to improved communication with staff and feedback mechanisms
- Continued regular consultation and negotiation with trade unions

CONCLUSION

"Let us ensure that as a result of SDR the conditions of service for our personnel are improved."

80. Defence depends on the people who provide it, Service and civilian. We intend to build on many of the policies we inherited but our Policy for People also pursues a series of new measures to address the issues raised with the liaison team during the consultation process. We are determined to put in place modern and fair policies which ensure that the Armed Forces and the MOD attract and retain the right people and truly reflect the society they serve.

SUPPORTING ESSAY TEN
PROCUREMENT AND INDUSTRY

1.   A central aim of the Strategic Defence Review is to ensure that the Armed Forces are properly equipped. We need to be able to undertake a wide variety of military tasks, from peacekeeping to high intensity conflict. This in turn carries a requirement for equipment that is inherently flexible. Ensuring that the right equipment is available in the right place at the right time is the job of the MOD acquisition staffs. Equipment acquisition is a pan-MOD activity involving the Central Staffs, the Procurement Executive, the Defence Evaluation and Research Agency and the Logistics Commands.

2.   Defence procurement has seen significant change over the last few years. New policies, procedures and ways of working have been introduced, such as competition, prime contractorship, pricing non-competitive contracts at the outset and collocation of the various elements of the Procurement Executive near Bristol. These have contributed to a more commercial relationship between the Department as customer and its suppliers. Many projects have run successfully on time and within budget, including the complex Trident submarine and missile programme.

3.   Unfortunately, however, annual examination by the National Audit Office (NAO) of the top 25 equipment programmes led them to report that, despite the changes, many major programmes suffer considerable time over-runs. Similarly, after some years of improving cost performance in the 1980s, recent NAO reports have recorded average overall cost over-runs of 7.5%-8.5% above original estimates (excluding Trident and Eurofighter) as shown in *FIGURE 1*.

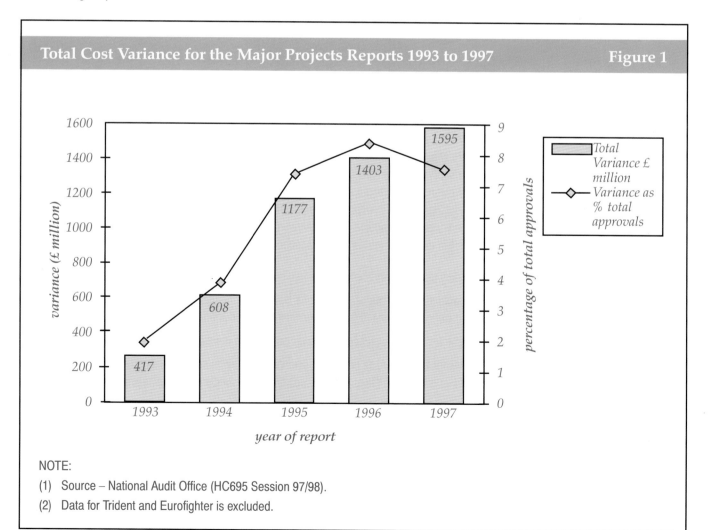

Total Cost Variance for the Major Projects Reports 1993 to 1997   **Figure 1**

NOTE:

(1)   Source – National Audit Office (HC695 Session 97/98).

(2)   Data for Trident and Eurofighter is excluded.

4.   The main causes of problems are:

–   slippage due to technical difficulties, budgetary constraints leading to the postponement of expenditure, the redefinition of requirements and difficulties over collaborative programmes;

–   cost over-runs due to programme changes, changes in equipment specification, poor estimating and inflation of prices for defence equipment in excess of inflation in the economy as a whole.

5.   Of these, technical difficulties are a major cause of delay. They arise from the complexity of modern defence equipment programmes which make them inherently risky. The current protracted procurement process does not easily provide for the incorporation of technical advances during the final stages of a project. Trying to rectify this by redefining the requirement during the life of the project tends only to bring about further delays and cost increases. Delays arising from collaboration usually occur at the key decision stages, when participating nations have to reconcile their own budgetary constraints and priorities.

6.   The Strategic Defence Review offered an opportunity to review the whole of the MOD's current equipment acquisition system, going back to first principles and examining every facet of our acquisition process with open minds. The Parliamentary criticisms formed a basis for this work. By discarding old practices which are no longer appropriate and learning from successful innovation in industry we have identified new ways of working and a new support organisation. As a result we are making radical changes, the most significant since the procurement organisations of the three Armed Services were brought together by the creation of the Procurement Executive in 1972. They will deliver a forward looking organisation using up to date acquisition processes and procedures. The emphasis will be on flexibility, in terms both of processes and organisation, and continuous evaluation to avoid any danger of stagnation.

Smart Procurement

7.   In July last year the Defence Secretary directed that the Strategic Defence Review should include a Smart Procurement Initiative. This initiative was a joint exercise with industry, under the auspices of the Defence Industries Council. It focused on processes rather than organisations and, in consultation with industry, produced a package of measures which acknowledges that procurement is a corporate process involving multiple stakeholders, including industry. Central to its findings is a 'Through Life Systems Approach' to procurement, which defines a new equipment or a new capability in the context of its relationship with other equipments and wider defence capability areas. A coherent process for co-ordinating a new equipment's requirement, linkage with the research programme, specification, acceptance and through-life management is a prerequisite for improved equipment acquisition.

8.   Smart Procurement means faster, cheaper and better. The key measures identified in the initiative included:

–   fuller early planning of projects with appropriate trade-offs between military requirements, time and costs, followed by more rapid, and hence cheaper, full development and production;

–   partnering arrangements with industry, particularly where competition is no longer viable;

–   exploitation of new procurement techniques including incremental acquisition (where a less ambitious initial capability is upgraded in lower risk steps) to be supported by concurrent engineering processes in industry;

–   improved estimating and predicting – integrated through-life cost forecasting utilising three-point estimating techniques should be applied to both time and cost and co-ordinated with the resource allocation and financial provision;

–   improved commercial practices – including measures to improve incentives for contractors, use of firm prices not subject to variation for contracts up to five years duration, greater consideration of contractor past performance in tender evaluation, new intellectual property rights conditions and greater use of electronic commerce;

The sum of these measures should be a new relationship between the Ministry of Defence and its suppliers in which both sides can operate to their strengths, under formal partnering arrangements where appropriate, and which provides industry with the greatest incentive to perform. It is through the establishment of such incentives that the customer/supplier relationship can best be improved to mutual advantage.

9.   Within the Strategic Defence Review, the Smart Procurement initiative included a fundamental re-examination of the acquisition process for the procurement of equipment for the Armed Forces. It looked at the way in which MOD is organised to conduct that process, and the value that each element of the organisation contributes to it.

10.   We analysed how processes in use across the MOD should be adapted to exploit the smart procurement tools and identified a number of organisational models for consideration. The roles of those who identify the requirements, procure the equipment and support it during its life have all been examined to see how any bottlenecks and unnecessary bureaucracy could be eliminated. Industry representatives were included in the mixed teams which carried out the studies. In all, some 22 industry representatives were involved alongside a MOD workforce of 43, together with nine from McKinsey, a firm of consultants.

11.   Mixed teams undertook a sequence of studies from which three specific concepts emerged (see *FIGURE 2*):

–   segmenting acquisition processes into three tiers with processes tailored to each; commodity/low risk items; minor projects and major projects (with collaboration as an important sub-set);

–   a single integrated project team bringing together all stakeholders and involving industry except during competition phases under the clear leadership of a team leader able to balance trade-offs between performance, cost and time within boundaries set by the approving authority;

–   the need to simplify approval processes and identify more precisely within the MOD the customer for the equipment.

High Level Processes   Figure 2

Strategy	▷	*Processes*	▷	*Organisation*
• *Clear segmentation of spend*		• *Revised front end process*		• *Clearly defined customer*
		• *Streamlined approvals and oversight*		• *Restructured acquisition organisation*
		• *Integrated Project Teams (IPTs)*		
		• *More effective positive and negative incentives*		

Segmented Acquisition Processes

12.   McKinsey's work confirmed how varied equipment acquisition has become. Three main categories of procurement were identified (see *FIGURE 3*), each absorbing roughly one third (£3Bn a year) of total equipment spending:

- **Tier I**. Items available in the market, often for non-defence application, such as standard vehicles and commodity items; the key characteristic is low technical risk and unit price. Defence items already developed (such as spares/support for existing equipment) are similar, although limited sources pose extra complexity for some of these items;

- **Tier II**. Defence specific items for which MOD needs to be an intelligent customer, but which are of intermediate scale and technical risk (e.g., a sub-system stand-alone weapon or an upgrade to an existing equipment not involving major systems integration);

- **Tier III**. The most complex systems, particularly platforms, which also require the integration of Tier I and II equipments and interaction with others. Key characteristics are high unit cost, substantial technical risk and limited sources of supply. Unless purchased off- the-shelf many will only be affordable if developed through an efficient collaborative process.

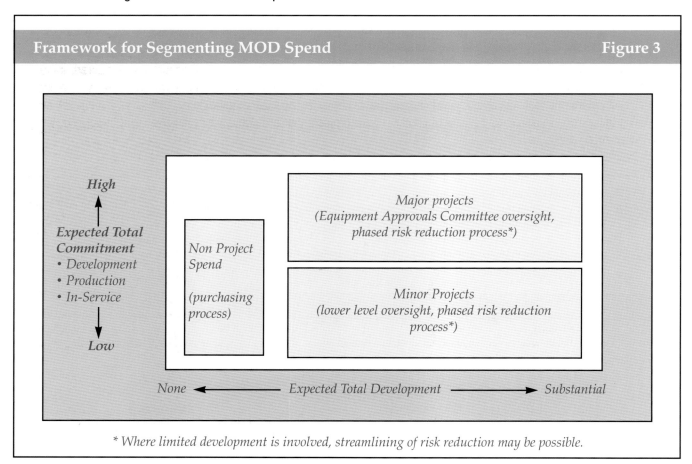

Framework for Segmenting MOD Spend   **Figure 3**

High

Expected Total
Commitment
• Development
• Production
• In-Service

Low

Non Project
Spend

(purchasing
process)

Major projects
(Equipment Approvals Committee oversight,
phased risk reduction process*)

Minor Projects
(lower level oversight, phased risk reduction
process*)

None ◄——— Expected Total Development ———► Substantial

* Where limited development is involved, streamlining of risk reduction may be possible.

13.   The studies suggested that significantly different processes are appropriate for these tiers. There are some common characteristics: defining military need, source selection, a contract or suitable equivalent; acceptance test; and public accountability. But substantially different depths of skill and breadth of view are needed between the different categories. The allocation to tiers does not judge relative importance: a minor item can be critical to military capability when incorporated in a larger system. It is the segmenting of processes that opens up the possibility of substantial gains. For example, one industry led group looked at simpler procedures for Tier I, such as using credit

cards or electronic bidding; whether there is a need for written contracts for smaller items; and the benefits of longer term supply arrangements.

14.   Historically, the functions of requirement definition, procurement management and through-life support have been organisationally separated. This has produced arms-length relationships between stakeholders which makes it difficult to get the right balance between time, risk, cost, performance and through-life support. There has also been an inherent optimism in predicting technical risk costs and time-scales. SDR work confirmed the desirability and feasibility from industrial experience of a much more integrated team approach, involving not only staff expert in military needs, technology, procurement and logistics, but also the industrial suppliers (though not during the competition phases). Experience in the US and in industry suggests that such teams can both promote a successful final outcome and offer major improvements in timescale and life-cycle cost. The MOD already has experience of such teams; its Trident team for example. There is however no guarantee of success; much depends on the calibre of the team leader and his/her authority both within the team and when dealing with industry and the customer. In future the leaders of the major project teams will be selected by competition, sometimes including candidates from outside the Department, and serve from four to five years.

Procedures

15.   The current process (known as the "Downey" Cycle) aims to control risk by a series of project stages with formal decision points between them. During the Cold War there was pressure for projects to be pushed forward into full development and production quickly so as to meet a specific Soviet threat, even though much risk remained: some ran into technical problems which caused delay. In the changed strategic environment we can take a different approach. More time can be taken for early concept and assessment phases, exploring options and reducing risk by testing technology (typically up to 15% of costs). Those projects that are chosen for full investment in subsequent demonstration and manufacturing phases will be better defined and involve lower risk and are thus more likely to run to planned time and cost. This different project cycle is illustrated in *FIGURE 4* below.

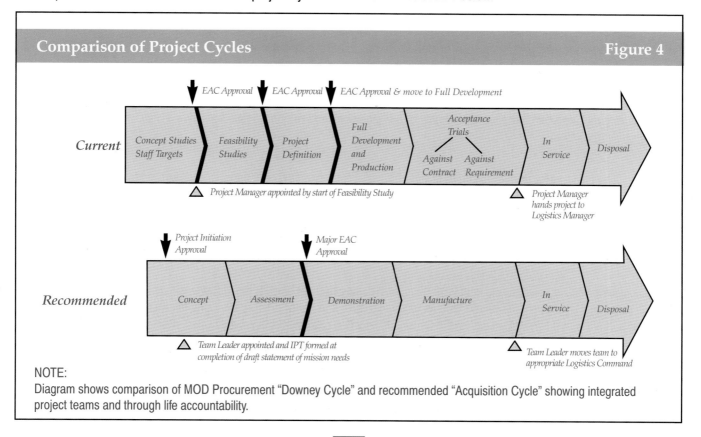

Comparison of Project Cycles   Figure 4

NOTE:
Diagram shows comparison of MOD Procurement "Downey Cycle" and recommended "Acquisition Cycle" showing integrated project teams and through life accountability.

16.   The existing approvals committee process will be modified and team leaders and customers will be able to take most decisions (with financial and technical scrutiny) but be held directly accountable for the consequences. Currently, equipment projects are formally approved at each stage in the Downey Cycle and, depending on their value, at a very senior level in the Department. While it is right, in view of the sums of money involved, for projects to be subject to regular scrutiny, the effect of the approvals process itself can be to extend the duration of a project. In future it is envisaged that projects should be subject to formal approvals normally twice only: at initiation, and prior to the main investment. Within such approvals, project team leaders will be empowered to make, and be held accountable for, trade-offs between time, risk, cost and performance. Ministers will continue to have visibility of all major or contentious projects.

Organisational Options

17.   Before considering organisational options, the Smart Procurement initiative went back to first principles and considered whether MOD needs to have a specialist procurement organisation or could safely leave the whole task to the private sector. Scope was identified for out-sourcing a larger proportion of the acquisition of routine items (e.g. a catalogue of pre-priced minor IT items and general stores) and specific functions. But it was concluded that for complex projects, MOD (like other managers of large projects) needs to keep core management in- house, while buying in specific skills.

18.   Various options were considered by Ministers for ownership of the Procurement Executive. The aim was to achieve greater clarity in customer/supplier relationships within the rest of MOD, and greater flexibility in personnel matters, whilst not reducing scope for personnel interchanges with the rest of MOD.

19.   The MOD procurement organisation needs to have a very close relationship with its military customers, capable of bringing together a wide range of interests using the 'single team' approach. While recognising that privatisation provides greater access to private sector expertise and incentives, industry felt it would be hard to reconcile with the single team approach. It was therefore concluded that procurement should remain as an in-house function of the MOD and that our requirements would be met most effectively by turning the Procurement Executive into a Defency Agency and by creating a single, central defence customer in MOD headquarters. Since the Procurement Executive already meets many of the technical requirements of an Agency we hope it will achieve this status by April 1999.

20.   The full benefits from these procurement process and organisational changes will take time to materialise, and are not solely financial. One of the principal objectives of these reforms is to prevent time and cost over-runs to ensure that the Armed Forces have the right equipment delivered at the right time and in some instances this will require a greater concentration of expenditure earlier in the procurement cycle. Capabilities may also need to be upgraded more regularly to keep pace with advances in technology.

21.   That said, significant and long term benefits are expected not only for the Department as customer but also for our suppliers. These can be summarised as faster, cheaper and better procurement and improved in-service support of equipment with down stream savings in through life costs. For example, initial estimates of potential acquisition cost benefits are in the region of £2Bn. The greatest impact of the reforms will be on procurements which are currently in their early formative stages and therefore most open to change, and the expected benefits will build up progressively as the process and organisational changes are established and applied to existing and new projects. This rolling process of continuous business improvement will need to be carried forward in conjunction with industry and also our major collaborative partners.

Commercial Relationship with Industry

22.   Throughout the work on Smart Procurement, the importance of a closer working relationship between MOD and industry has been emphasised. It is seen as a necessary precursor to a more efficient and effective procurement regime. Both sides acknowledged that for many the current relationship was often perceived as adversarial, caused by a lack of mutual understanding and trust.

23.   The successful working relationships that have been forged during the Smart Procurement initiative, and which are already in existence in some project areas, will therefore be encouraged, sustained and expanded. This will be done through a number of routes, including: joint training, enhanced interchange programmes, and inclusion of industry representatives on integrated teams.

24.   Care will be taken to ensure that closer links with industry are taken forward under clear guidelines that preserve the formal and overarching accountabilities of the Department for the integrity of the procurement process and the protection of public funds.

Making it Happen

25.   In order to ensure that the changes are carried through in an efficient and effective manner a range of implementation measures has been agreed. Among the key elements are:

- a full-time implementation team including industry and limited consultancy support. This will not be another unnecessary layer of bureaucracy. Evidence from previous exercises of this kind is that implementation teams stimulate and assist change;

- development of an acquisition stream for both military and civilian staff which would provide core personnel for the Integrated Project Teams. This will be supported by training and personal development and there will be increased interchanges with industry; it should be a two way process with people from industry spending time in MOD;

- close definition and monitoring of processes backed by clear performance measures;

- a continued Ministerial lead.

A Specialist Stream of Acquisition Personnel in MOD

26.   Personnel, training and staff development issues were considered as part of the review of the procurement organisation, with the emphasis on the need to support the new proposed processes and Integrated Project Teams. A clear requirement emerged for the formation of a broad Acquisition stream, encompassing military and civilian staff involved in the full spectrum of the defence procurement process, from the earliest stages of requirement formulation to the final disposal of obsolete equipment. It will cover the current operational requirements, procurement management, contracts, finance and logistics functions.

27.   Fundamental to the Acquisition stream will be the definition of a comprehensive set of competences. As well as specific professional skills, these will include people skills such as team-working, communications and leadership. In parallel, schemes such as the new post graduate Systems Engineering degree course at Shrivenham, staff development schemes, and interchange and secondment programmes will be developed to support an acquisition career, and equip staff to meet the needs of the new processes and organisations. Much of the training will be undertaken jointly with industry.

Britain's Defence Industrial Base

28.   In its Manifesto the Government stated that "we support a strong UK defence industry which is a strategic part of our industrial base as well as our defence effort". The way in which we have involved industry in the Strategic Defence Review demonstrates our commitment to this statement. A strong industrial base underpins a robust defence policy, so the success of both customer and supplier are closely intertwined.

29.   Following the Defence Secretary's request for inputs to the Strategic Defence Review in July of last year and after wide consultation within the defence industry, the Defence Industries Council[1] submitted a paper entitled *"Strength Through Partnership"* in October 1997. Individual submissions to the Strategic Defence Review were also made directly from companies within the defence sector.

30.   Defence export orders have reached over £5Bn per annum. They are beneficial not just to Britain's economy, but directly to the MOD. Savings to MOD through reduced fixed overhead charges resulting from exports amount to some £350M per year. In addition, the MOD also benefits through receipts from Commercial Exploitation Levy payments for the use of products whose development it has funded. These receipts have averaged some £50M per year over the last five years. The competitiveness of the defence sector, proven by its record of success in overseas markets, further helps to demonstrate the efficiency and effectiveness of those who supply and increasingly support our operations in the field.

Industrial Capabilities

31.   The MOD is not alone in its recognition of the need to react to changing circumstances. The defence industrial base that supports Britain's military capabilities is also changing in response to both technological and commercial pressures. The traditional distinction between the civil and defence industrial sectors has been eroded by the increasing importance for defence purposes of technologies of civil origin; developments in electronics and information technology illustrate the point, which applies equally to our allies, that we can no longer think in terms of a defence-unique industrial base.

32. At the same time, defence industry and the defence market has become more internationalised, a trend which looks set to go further. Ownership of the defence industry is becoming more multi-national. Such supply-side developments are consistent with the emphasis in our own plans, and those of our partners, on collaborative procurement.

33.   These changes are bringing about an increased level of mutual interdependence in the procurement and support of equipment. Neither we, nor our partners retain indigenously the full range of capabilities to which we need access. This more complex industrial setting makes it all the more important to take careful account of the industrial implications of the available options when taking procurement decisions. We remain committed to securing the best value for money, and each procurement decision will therefore be assessed on its merits, with industrial aspects being assessed against a range of defence based criteria. These include maintaining an ability for industry to support military operations and to regenerate critical equipment stocks, as well as other considerations, such as exports, collaboration and sustaining the future scope for competition.

---

1 The Defence Industries Council is the collective term for those individual industrialists and representatives of the four major defence trade associations (the Society of British Aerospace Companies, Defence Manufacturers Association, Federation of the Electronics Industry and British Naval Equipment Association) who represent industry's views on the National Defence Industries Council chaired by the Secretary of State for Defence. This is the primary vehicle through which the MOD consults the defence industries on matters of common interest.

Defence Industry Restructuring

34. With some 40% of output based on exports British companies must remain competitive in world markets to ensure their survival and commercial well being. The need for consolidation in Europe to maintain global competitiveness has been recognised for some time and is increasingly urgent. Our acceptance of this commercial reality is not at odds with our commitment to a strong defence industry; indeed, we see restructuring as an essential part of achieving this objective. Industry must restructure if it is to prosper in the face of competition from the US "defence giants", and if it is to be able to co-operate with the US from a position of strength.

35. The Prime Minister, together with President Chirac and Chancellor Khol, gave fresh impetus to the restructuring process in a trilateral statement which was issued on 9 December 1997. This called on industry to present their plans for industrial restructuring by 31 March 1998. The four Airbus partners (British Aerospace, Aerospatiale, DASA and CASA) responded to this challenge by presenting a joint report on 27 March. This indicates that the companies have reached broad agreement that the target structure should be a single, integrated European Aerospace and Defence Company. We welcome the broad measure of agreement reached.

36. Whilst detailed restructuring plans must be led by industry, we recognise that governments can help to facilitate such developments. As a major customer of the defence industry, we must keep them informed about our future programmes to provide a sound basis for commercial decisions. The Strategic Defence Review has set out to achieve this for Britain. And we can negotiate international agreements to underpin restructuring. In the short term, these include issues such as: security of supply, security of information, export procedures, research and technology funding, and intellectual property rights. These issues are to be addressed within a Letter of Intent which we anticipate will receive Ministerial agreement in July 1998. Italy and Spain have now joined these discussions, and we are proceeding on a five nation basis.

Collaboration

37. International collaboration is of increasing importance to our forward equipment programme. It offers tangible military, economic and industrial benefits and it is essential that the UK remains at the forefront of developments in this area of joint endeavour. We continue to work actively within NATO and with our partners in the Western European Armaments Group, which operates within the framework of the Western European Union, to identify opportunities for collaboration, promote a stronger European Research effort, establish a more open and competitive market for defence equipment in Europe and address many of the difficult issues concerning the European defence technological and industrial base.

38. British membership of Organisme Conjointe de Co-operation en matiere d'Armament (OCCAR), the quadrilateral armament structure with France, Germany and Italy, also presents a real opportunity to establish with our major European partners improved collaborative practices which deliver value for money products able to compete effectively in world markets. Our work on 'Smart Procurement' should be beneficial to such a process. We remain fully committed to the pursuit of common OCCAR objectives – which includes the extension of membership to other states and the establishment of a 'legal personality' – with our current partners.

Conclusion

39.   The MOD must procure the equipment the Armed Forces need, when they need it. We must ensure that the Services have equipment which is capable, reliable, and durable. It must be procured in time, and to cost; to do otherwise, as has happened all too often in the past, would be letting down not only our Service men and women, but also the taxpayer. A radical initiative was clearly needed, and has produced a blueprint for a better way of procuring defence equipment. We now have the means at our disposal to ensure that, in future, the Services have the capability they need, and taxpayers the value-for-money they deserve.

SUPPORTING ESSAY ELEVEN
SUPPORT AND INFRASTRUCTURE

Introduction

1.   From the outset, the Government made it clear that the Strategic Defence Review would be policy-led, not resource-driven. But this did not mean that resources could be disregarded. On the contrary, it was recognised that a crucial element of the Review would be a comprehensive re-examination of every area of defence business, to ensure that the defence capabilities required by our policy objectives are generated as cost-effectively and efficiently as possible. As the Defence Secretary put it in his speech to the Royal United Services Institute on 18 September 1997:

"The Strategic Defence Review will be seeking to ensure that, as far as humanly practicable, every pound spent on defence will be spent both wisely and well."

2.   This general duty to the taxpayer was reinforced by the specific imperative to identify savings which would enable us to repair inherited gaps in capability, as well as to meet emerging requirements identified in the Review. Accordingly, a dedicated strand of the Review was established to find the maximum possible level of efficiency savings by thoroughly scrutinising, in particular, defence support and infrastructure.

3.   The detailed results of the work undertaken are described below. Overall the exercise succeeded both in achieving significant new savings to help rectify capability deficiencies identified elsewhere in the Review process, and in putting in place a series of system and organisational improvements that will pay continuing dividends in the future.

Context

4.   The drive for efficiency in the conduct of MOD's business is not new. Since the end of the Cold War, defence has had to adapt to managing within a budget now 29% smaller in real terms than in the mid-1980s. This meant a sustained and continuing effort to drive down operating costs, reduce overheads and maximise the output of effective defence capability from the provision available. The main features of this effort have been:

-   a complete re-design of the Department's management and budgetary structure;

-   a series of specific efficiency reviews, notably the Defence Costs Study of 1994 which took over £1Bn a year out of support costs;

-   the biggest Market Testing and Contracting Out programme in government;

-   a major Private Finance Initiative programme, developing increasingly innovative forms of partnership with the private sector;

-   headquarters reduction which has cut London based personnel by 60% since 1990, and reduced the Department's core headquarters staff by over 30%;

-   an annual efficiency planning system covering all operating costs and fully integrated with the resource allocation system;

-   efficiency savings which have now accumulated since the end of the 1980s to over £4Bn annually.

5.   The Review has built on these foundations, and complemented them with a series of important new proposals for change. Work on defence assets has proved particularly fruitful. Previously, relatively little management attention had been paid to the cost of owning capital assets, which was not apparent under cash accounting. The imminent introduction of commercial-style accounts throughout MOD, and the preparatory work to draw up balance-sheets, provided an invaluable point of departure for the comprehensive studies of defence asset holdings described below.

Approach to the Efficiency and Assets Work

6.   At the start of the Efficiency and Assets workstage of the Review, all of the Ministry of Defence's 13 main operating divisions ('Top Level Budgets') were required to conduct thorough business analyses of their management areas, and to draw up Management and Efficiency Audit Reports. The purpose of this was to look radically at the scope for providing the same output for less resources. Management areas were also required to review their asset holdings and consider the scope for reduction or better utilisation. Another major theme was the promotion of Public Private Partnerships - identification of new ways of working with the private sector in more cost-effective arrangements for meeting defence requirements. And, across the board, management areas were tasked to consider the scope for slimming management hierarchies and reducing overheads.

7.   The response was impressive. Inherited forward efficiency plans already envisaged that, over the four years from 1998/99, considerable new efficiency gains would be achieved. As a result of this exercise, the planned efficiency achievement across the Department was more than doubled.

8.   This, however, was only the first step. Ideas on how to further improve efficiency were invited from MOD Service and civilian personnel, and the views of the Trades Unions and industry were canvassed. External involvement was an important feature of the work, and a number of outside experts contributed generous help to the various different strands of the work. Proposals, too, came forward from the main operating divisions for efficiency improvements with wider implications going beyond the competence of their particular areas.

9.   Accordingly, the 'bottom-up' approach of the Management and Efficiency Audit Reports was complemented by a series of wide- ranging 'top-down' studies. Most ran across organisational boundaries and particular emphasis was laid on developing new joint approaches – as between the three Services, and their civilian counterparts where relevant. In many areas, this was the key to increasing both efficiency and effectiveness, and to eliminating unnecessary duplication and overhead. Indeed, the Defence Secretary established the presumption that services should be provided and functions carried out on a joint basis, unless there were good reasons for continued management on single-Service lines.

10.   The major elements of this area of work fell into the four broad categories discussed below. Associated work on improving MOD's procurement of equipment and materiel, and restructuring our procurement organisations, is covered in the separate essay on "Procurement and Industry".

Assets

11.   Fighting equipment apart, the MOD's principal assets comprise land and buildings, and stocks. Comprehensive reviews of both areas were carried out and identified major savings.

Review of the Defence Estate

12.   The MOD is a major land-owner in Britain. The majority of our holdings are training land, which is heavily utilised and remains at a premium. But we also occupy a built estate of some 80,000 hectares. Properties worth about £700M have been sold since 1990, in addition to the sale of the married quarters estate. Despite these significant disposals, the Review began with a presumption that rigorous scrutiny could identify scope for additional receipts and reducing running costs. All parts of the Department, the Treasury and the Cabinet Office Efficiency Unit contributed to this work, together with private sector advice, particularly on the management of the estate.

13.   **Major disposals.** Our re-examination of the defence estate should enable us to double the inherited programme for disposal receipts over the next four years to more than £700M. The Review focused on higher value properties, particularly in London. Our 100 highest value sites across the country were reviewed thoroughly. Most meet long-term operational requirements and cannot be economically replaced elsewhere, but all will be kept under review. Of the London sites:

- the Duke of York's Headquarters in Chelsea, principally occupied by the Territorial, Auxiliary & Volunteer Reserve Association for Greater London and Territorial Army units, will be sold and its occupants re-accommodated as necessary;

- Chelsea barracks needs to be replaced (not necessarily on its present site) and this will be achieved through a Public Private Partnership project;

- the Millbank barracks site is also included in the disposals programme, as are a number of smaller London sites;

- London headquarters office buildings have already reduced from 25 in 1993 to seven today, and will now reduce to just two (the Whitehall Main Building and the Old War Office Building) by 2004, when Main Building redevelopment has been completed.

14. Further reductions in land and buildings in the London area should be possible and we are drawing up a strategic development plan. We shall be considering in particular our future requirements at RAF Northolt and RAF Uxbridge and a number of other major sites in the Greater London area.

15.   Elsewhere, significant estate sales now planned include parts of the Army sites at Chilwell and Woolwich; storage and support sites at Didcot, Malvern, Old Dalby, Thatcham and RAF Cardington; parts of Defence Evaluation and Research Agency sites at Bromley, Chertsey (north site) and Farnborough (Queen's Gate); and office accommodation in the Bath area. In addition, we expect to make reductions in the estate occupied by the Territorial Army in line with the reductions in its personnel numbers.

16.   In total, over 350 separate sites, ranging from major establishments to small parcels of land identified as surplus, are included in the forward disposal programme. A check is made for each site before it is put on the market to ensure that there is no suitable alternative defence use for it. Where our estate plans have significant implications for civilian staff, the Trade Unions have been or will be consulted.

17.   Taken together, the planned programme of disposals will bring the total reduction in the size of our built estate in the United Kingdom since 1990 to some 20% – about the same as the percentage reduction over that period in the numbers of Service and civilian personnel based throughout the country.

18.   **Training Land**. About two-thirds of the defence estate by area is rural training land. A shortfall in the land available to meet military training requirements had been identified before the Review began. We do not expect there to be scope for any overall reduction, but the implications of the Review for military training will now be considered in detail. Environmental appraisal will form an integral part of the process to inform our future strategy for the size and utilisation of the rural estate. Environmental and conservation groups were consulted during the Review and their views will be sought in developing our strategy. We shall also honour our existing commitments to consult with the relevant statutory bodies about changes in land use that may be proposed. The Army's Land Command continues to improve its arrangements for the efficient utilisation and management of the estate, and we are considering the scope for greater involvement of the private sector.

19.   **Management of the Estate**. The Review identified a need for central strategic management of the defence estate, to ensure that it is managed efficiently and cost-effectively as a coherent whole; that the pressure to reduce holdings is maintained; and that we derive maximum value for money from our expenditure on property maintenance

and capital works. Top level budget holders will remain individually accountable for the property that they occupy and for funding it, but the Chief Executive of the Defence Estates agency will be held accountable for the management of the estate as a whole; he will manage the disposals programme; and his team will provide an improved professional interface with industry.

20.   Estate strategy will be overseen by the Defence Estates Board, chaired by the Parliamentary Under Secretary of State. The strategy will bring together forward plans; keep existing uses and utilisation of the estate under review; and enable us to identify further opportunities for disposals and for sharing between Service users. This will include concentrating smaller units on larger multi-user core sites, where cost-effective and appropriate.

Review of Stockholdings

21. Defence stockholdings have been substantially reduced in recent years:

- since 1990, £4.4Bn of stock has been sent for disposal;

- the number of individual types of item held has been cut from three to two million;

- 50 out of 81 depots have closed.

22.   But stock retained totals £8Bn of missiles and ammunition, and £11Bn of other items (mainly spares and items in the repair loop). These holdings will be reviewed against the principles that stocks should be held only where they cannot be obtained within readiness preparation times for operations; and that operational stocks should not be maintained in excess of realistic operational need or deployment plans. Major savings targets have been identified through disposing of surplus stocks and improved processes to reduce the procurement of new stock:

- existing plans for review and disposal of redundant stock can be expanded and accelerated;

- flexible provisioning methods taking full account of the costs of holding stock are likely to allow more of our requirements for peacetime provisioning and for training to be met by direct supply from industry, permanently reducing our need to hold stock.

23.   Against that background, a new reduction target of 20% in the book value of stockholdings (other than ammunition and missiles) over the next three years has been set. This amounts to £2.2Bn. A separate study will consider the scope for contractorisation of the management of clothing supply.

24.   The market value of disposals will be slight. But stock reductions on this scale will allow further reductions in storage and distribution infrastructure (described more fully at paragraph 40).

25.   **Future provisioning**. The Review considered how far savings in future provisioning could be achieved. Some stock is systematically held to cover production line inefficiencies, administrative, transport or other delays, or inaccurate provisioning calculations. We concluded that there is scope for considerable saving if radical business efficiency measures, building on plans already being developed, are introduced.

26.   Much progress on these lines was already assumed in MOD's forward plans. Forward financial provision has already been reduced in anticipation of new efficiencies of this kind. But the Review nonetheless concluded that further savings would be practicable and that additional targets should be imposed.

27.   **War reserves**. As a result of longer post-Cold War readiness preparation times, there is now scope for reducing holdings of war reserves such as guided weapons and ammunition. The key to reducing stocks and hence financial provision is an appreciation of the critical factors in production lead times. If new production lead times can

be brought below readiness preparation time, by stocking long-lead components and materials rather than complete weapons, paying manufacturers for dormant production capability, or other partial investments, stock procurement can be reduced and economies (for example in the disposal and replacement of life-expired stocks) can be made. Studies will be conducted with industry on individual production lines as soon as practicable.

Defence Organisation

28.   A series of organisational studies was undertaken during the Review, aimed at rationalisation, reduction of overheads and reinforcing joint approaches wherever this makes operational sense. These latter aspects are also considered in the essay on joint operations.

29.   At the highest level, we considered whether current arrangements (themselves only recently evolved from the reorganisations of the early 1990s) represent the optimum balance between single Service organisations (through which front line force elements are necessarily and rightly generated) and cross-defence structures embodying the joint approach.

30.   **Joint Operations**. Building on the success of the Permanent Joint Headquarters, we have decided to enhance the role and responsibilities of the Chief of Joint Operations, including making him responsible for a top-level budget and thus putting him on the same budgetary footing as the single Service Commanders in Chief.

31. **Defence Logistics**. Careful consideration was given to our arrangements for the provision of logistics support to the front line. The current position, with three single-Service logistics organisations, ensures the necessary close relationship between the logistics area and the front-line forces it supports, but it is less well suited to maximising the scope for rationalisation and convergence on a functional, defence-wide basis. Our work also took account of the demands of operations, which are increasingly conducted on a joint basis with units of two or three Services working closely alongside each other. As a result of the Review, we have decided that:

- the three single-Service logistics organisations will be brought together into a unified organisation to provide logistic support to all three Services;

- a Chief of Defence Logistics (a four-star uniformed post) will be appointed to take overall control of the current organisations and re-configure them, after an appropriate transition period, into one integrated organisation which will, however, retain the necessary close relationship with front-line forces;

- amongst other advantages, this will facilitate the achievement of important benefits flowing from the Smart Procurement initiative across the logistics area.

32.   **Joint Defence Centre**. A single authority will be established for the formation and development of joint and single Service doctrine, in the shape of a new Joint Defence Centre.

33.   **Headquarters**. All these developments will have a significant impact on the Department's headquarters. This needs more time to work through. But a number of key decisions have already been taken:

- elevation of the Chief of Joint Operations to Top Level Budget Holder status will transfer some £300M of annual operating costs from the two Centre Top Level Budgets;

- the remainder will be better managed as one consolidated Top Level Budget covering all central headquarters costs, and expenditure on corporate, defence-wide services and functions which it makes sense to hold centrally. Such services range from the joint medical agencies, through the Ministry of Defence Police to pay and personnel administration;

- this will create a central Top Level Budget controlling a little over £2Bn of operating costs a year, with headquarters costs of about £170M separately identifiable within it.

34.   Working through the implications of these various changes should result in a slimmer central organisation for defence, which can be accommodated after the redevelopment of the Main Building in only two London buildings. This will allow the release of one further office building, over and above previous plans.

35.   Meanwhile, some small but useful staff reductions have been identified in headquarters areas such as research management, central warfare staff, environmental and health and safety policy, and information and communications services. In particular, a review of the Defence Intelligence Staff (in London and Agencies, and in their interfaces with the Commands) has identified significant savings.

36.   **Army Land Command Restructuring**. Land Command is currently consulting on a proposal to re-shape the Army's administrative structure in the United Kingdom. The present structure was established in part to reflect the needs of military home defence, which have changed fundamentally. Land Command proposes that the current six divisions/districts would be replaced for administration purposes by three. Depending on the detailed outcome, establishment closures or reductions may result at a number of locations.

37.   **Territorial, Auxiliary and Volunteer Reserve Associations (TAVRAs).** Following a review of the structures through which the Volunteer Reserves and Cadets are administered, a number of changes have been proposed including reduction of the number of TAVRAs from 14 to 12 to bring them into line with the Land Command brigade structure. This will require secondary legislation. These changes will produce a clearer and more coherent framework for linking the administration of Regular and Reserve forces.

Logistics

38.   Much progress has been made in recent years in rationalising logistic support to the Armed Forces, often within a Defence Agency framework:

  – "lead-Service" arrangements operate widely. For example, the Royal Navy procures food on behalf of all three Services;

  – private sector involvement is already extensive.

39.   We considered how present arrangements might be improved, to better meet the requirements of joint and force projection operations, and to take forward rationalisation and business practice improvements on a joint basis. The most significant outcome of this work was the decision to unify the three single-Service logistics organisations under a new Chief of Defence Logistics (paragraph 31 above). But a series of other important changes were also decided upon, as described below.

40.   **Storage and Distribution**. We plan to form a single, defence- wide, storage and distribution Defence Agency in the early years of the next century:

  – as a first step it is planned to form a Defence Storage and Distribution Agency (Non-explosive), on a lead-Service basis by the Quartermaster General, by April 1999. This will replace the current single-Service arrangements and should produce substantial efficiency savings;

  – work on explosive storage processing and distribution, currently split between the Royal Navy and Army, recommended unifying the explosives storage function as a division of the existing Naval Bases and Supply Agency by April 1999;

  – creation of the final unified organisation, to perform all storage and distribution tasks, is envisaged for 2004/05. En route, additional consideration will be given to the scope for further private sector involvement in the task.

41.   We intend to consult on plans for the early closure of the Royal Navy Stores Depots at Rosyth and Colerne, and envisage that the stock reduction programme (para 22 above) should enable us to reduce storage capacity by the equivalent of a further major depot in the early years of the next decade.

42.   **Fuels and Lubricants**. As a result of the work on fuels and lubricants the procurement and management of all MOD fuels and lubricants will be conducted on a lead-Service basis (by the Royal Air Force), with the exception of naval "bespoke fuels" which will initially continue to be managed separately. Fuel reserve stocks will also be significantly reduced. In addition, commercial best practice, benchmarking and other improvements to the management of fuel procurement will be adopted.

43.   The Government Pipeline and Storage System (GPSS) is currently managed by the Oil and Pipeline Agency (a Non-Departmental Public Body). A study was conducted to consider the potential benefits of increased private sector involvement in utilising and managing the system. Much of this work was performed by outside consultants, who recommended greater commercial exploitation via a partnering arrangement with a major oil company and/or a long-term concession. Expressions of interest have been received. Other elements of the non-GPSS fuels infrastructure will be rationalised allowing disposals of some assets.

44.   **Strategic Movements**. Large-scale movements of people and materiel are currently managed by several different staffs and authorities. Study work concluded that efficiency and effectiveness would both be improved by rationalising the relevant staffs (including the Defence Transport and Movements Executive, which currently has responsibility for land and sea movements, but not air). We therefore intend to create a Defence Transport and Movements Agency in April 1999, to be overseen by the Quartermaster General on the lead-Service principle.

45.   **Commercial utilisation.** Further work explored the scope for increasing the commercial utilisation of MOD's movements infrastructure, particularly the Marchwood Military Port. Scope was identified to generate revenue within the existing operation at Marchwood, and to pursue a partnering arrangement (which might involve a commercial partner sharing in the port's operation, possibly using Sponsored Reserves – employees of the commercial partner prepared to be deployed forward to operational theatres when required).

46.   **Logistics Processes and Information Technology Systems Convergence**. This study reviewed the business processes for logistic provisioning and the information systems which support them. Important progress was made on a strategy to align the business practices and IT systems of the three single-Service logistics organisations. This will underpin the other SDR logistics proposals and will be fundamental to achieving the benefits and savings of the Smart Procurement initiative (see the 'Procurement and Industry' essay) and the work on stockholdings.

47.   **Defence Aviation Repair Agency**. Major repair and overhaul of military aircraft is currently carried out by two separate Defence Agencies, one for helicopters and another for fixed-wing aircraft. As announced by the Minister for the Armed Forces on 23 April, we have decided to bring these two operations together in a single Defence Agency, the Defence Aviation Repair Agency. Given the major efficiency programmes already underway in each of the two existing Agencies, only modest overhead savings can initially be assumed. But we intend to move the new organisation to Trading Fund status as soon as possible, with the expectation of further efficiency gains from operation in a more commercial environment.

48.   **Army Equipment Support**. The Army's head of logistic support, the Quartermaster General, is developing proposals for a major re-shaping of the Army's equipment support function. Operational, technical, contract and financial staff will be integrated to form multi-disciplinary groups managing equipment support. Reduction and relocation of staffs will be involved, as well as the absorption of the Army Technical Support Agency into the new organisation. The Army Base Repair Organisation will be restructured, with a view to moving it to Trading Fund status.

Agencies

49.   Most of Defence support is now delivered through 44 Defence Agencies. A number of Agencies have achieved savings on their operating costs of over 20% in their first two or three years and several of the programmes involve rationalisation of activities from anything up to 20 sites to a single location. The Agencies are principal contributors to the Department's efficiency programme, achieving rates around double that of the rest of the Department. They also play a leading role in the development of increasingly innovative forms of Public Private Partnerships. Many of the Defence Agencies will be affected by SDR outcomes detailed above, which include the formation of new Agencies in such areas as aviation repair, strategic movements, storage and distribution and, probably, Army equipment support.

50.   **Agency management.** In common with other Government Departments, we are developing the ways in which Agencies' output objectives are specified, to build a management environment in which the Chief Executives enjoy maximum freedom to achieve these objectives, and are fully held to account for doing so. Particular attention will be paid to this agenda in the wake of the Review, including pursuit of a campaign to recruit external advisers as non-executive members of Defence Agency Boards. A range of actions is in place to carry this forward, including the preparation of fresh guidance to Agency "owners" (the senior officials to whom, under Ministers, the Chief Executive is accountable). This will reflect the Department's experience to date. Training programmes will be redesigned to alter the focus from establishing Agencies to managing them, both internally and at the level of the Owner. Arrangements for sharing best practice have also been set in place, with a series of seminars to bring together owners, customers and Chief Executives.

51.   **The Defence Evaluation and Research Agency (DERA).** DERA is MOD's largest Agency, operating as a Trading Fund with 12,500 staff and an annual turn-over of some £1Bn. We will harness the opportunities offered by a Public Private Partnership to strengthen DERA's ability to continue to provide world class scientific research well into the next century.

Conclusion

52.   The Review of Support and Infrastructure has been comprehensive and far-reaching:

- the first phase of the exercise resulted in a doubling of MOD's projected future efficiency achievement;

- the Department has set itself the challenge of securing annual accumulating efficiency gains of 3% in our operating costs over the next four years; and

- major steps have been taken to increase the joint approach in the support area.

53.   Achieving 3% is a challenging target which will require us to identify new efficiency gains in the years ahead in addition to the measures identified in the Review. But on the basis of the major advances identified in the Review, the target should be achievable. This planned efficiency gain is over and above the increased receipts expected from estate disposals and the efficiencies resulting from the Smart Procurement initiative, which is described in another essay.

54.   The introduction of commercial-style accounting will maintain the momentum imparted by the Review to the reduction and maximum utilisation of defence assets. New arrangements for the strategic management of the estate should enable us to ensure a continuing process of rationalisation and reduction in our holdings of land and buildings; and the development of our approach to the management of Defence Agencies should likewise pay continuing dividends over the years ahead.

55.   The twin aims of the efficiency and assets workstage of the Strategic Defence Review were:

–   to identify savings in the defence budget to help repair inherited capability deficiencies; and

–   to put in place system improvements that would pay continuing dividends in the future.

56.   In both respects it was successful; significant savings have been identified, and a wide variety of improvements have been set in train which will stand the Ministry of Defence in good stead well into the next century.